FINDING
YOUR WAY

To my Dear Friend
mandy
who I treasure as a
friend.
Thank you for being
my friend
Love Ethna
2021

This book is dedicated to my husband, Martin,
and my daughters, Clare and Siobhán.

To the friends and family who have walked with me.

And to all the tourists who long to be pilgrims.

ELIZABETH
McKENNA

EDITED BY MARIA McGUINNESS

FINDING
YOUR WAY

The Joy of the Camino

First published in 2019 by
Elizabeth McKenna
Glasnevin
Dublin 11
Ireland

Paperback	ISBN: 978 1 78846 1115
eBook – mobi format	ISBN: 978 1 78846 1122
eBook – ePub format	ISBN: 978 1 78846 1139
Amazon paperback edition	ISBN: 978 1 78846 1146

Produced by Kazoo Independent Publishing Services
222 Beech Park, Lucan, Co. Dublin
www.kazoopublishing.com

Kazoo Independent Publishing Services is not the publisher of this work. All rights and responsibilities pertaining to this work remain with Elizabeth McKenna.

Kazoo offers independent authors a full range of publishing services. For further details visit www.kazoopublishing. com

Cover design by Andrew Brown

Printed in the EU

Contents

'Empathy for people is the way to live and forgiveness is the way to heal.
We all need healing.'

— ELIZABETH MCKENNA

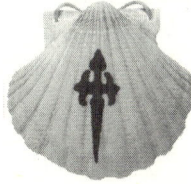

Preface

During the Middle Ages when people needed to rectify 'choices', some went on a pilgrimage seeking a 'plenitude indulgence'. The Road of St James to Santiago de Compostela is one of the most important Christian pilgrimages. It is known as the 'Way of Saint James'. Although it begins on your own doorstep, the official routes start in many countries, including Germany, Holland, Portugal, France, Ireland and England. They all finish in the cathedral in Santiago de Compostela, in Galicia, north-western Spain. Legend has it St James's remains were carried by boat from Jerusalem. His remains were recovered there and a cathedral was built in the city of Santiago de Compostela. His body now lies in a casket in a tomb in the cathedral. This cathedral is visited by pilgrims of all backgrounds, regardless of religious beliefs. They walk, run, cycle and some even go on horseback or donkeys. Many undertake the Camino simply because they feel pulled to it, led to it for various reasons, some known and personal, others completely unknown. Many have no idea why they have found themselves on that road, but they do, and for many, those reasons make themselves known eventually. The goal is to reach the cathedral and to challenge yourself en route.

Every road can be a Camino, just as life itself is. In this book I detail a number of Caminos, including one in the Himalayas. Caminos are not easy; there are twists and turns, ups and downs – but also great joy.

With courage and an open mind one can charge fearlessly through the excitement and mystery. We are all given the gift of life and a choice in how to live it.

This book presents a journey within a journey, none of which was intentional. It all started with a few words in a diary. I was amazed at the daily journey and the help received while en route, sometimes in extreme circumstances, where the outcome could have been catastrophic without divine intervention. Dreams and messages from the guides that I call angels sent me in a twirl of wonder. For some time now, I have been documenting events and promising I would make a story and share it. I have linked all my journeys in the hope of presenting a conclusion, some clarity on what I was meant to find and to understand. I could not have done this without the help of my friends and soulmates who travelled with me, unaware of my deep feelings and at times tormented nights trying to piece together the messages within my dreams.

Before undertaking this piece of writing, I was told, not once but three times, that I would be writing these things down. Three different people told me, including two psychics I just happened to see in Scotland by coincidence. One told me about Santiago de Compostela before I knew anything about this place and the significance of the journey on people's lives. The third was Aidan Story – a man in Ireland that communicates with the angels and has written his own story. He was adamant I was to do this, and that I would be directed to the right place and the right person would help me when the time was right. In the summer of 2015, I visited a spiritual psyche medium. My friend Lesley, another person who hears and acknowledges the angel's messages, said I should see her and so we went together. Vivienne told me there were saints, spirits and Our Lady Mary walking with me into her room. I had been writing about the saints I encountered on my travels and I was very surprised to hear her tell me about Our Lady. I always pray to her and have always wondered if she was around me on my journeys. Vivienne spoke of the saints, whose presence I feel regularly. She mentioned a person around me that had passed away suddenly from a heart complaint. I thought it was my brother until I was walking out the door and she said, raising her hands in the air, 'onwards and upwards'. I looked at her in astonishment, as there was only one person I knew who always said that – my friend Vinney. He had passed away eight months earlier, six months after my brother from the same ailment.

Finding Your Way

I was told in a dream shortly after that visit that there were three angels sent to help me with this writing. 'No more Caminos,' they said, and the angels handed me what looked like an open book. I was being told to put pen to paper. Shortly after that dream, while in a church in Dublin, I was handed a picture of three angels by a complete stranger. The first was St Michael, God's right-hand man who protects us from evil. The second was St Gabriel, the angel of communication, and the third angel was St Raphael whose name means 'God heals'. The very next day, my sister, Kathy, handed me a book by Doreen Virtue on St Gabriel.

We are all on a Camino, depending on each other for support and guidance. From the time I was seven years old, my trust in God and the angels was just something I always acknowledged to myself, automatically thanking them for their help. I would make my way to the church, sometimes I would attend Mass, other times I'd spend time looking at the statues and wondering who they were. I always felt safe there. I always thought it was the same for everyone, that we were all blessed with the angels. My adventures with friends by foot and by bike have taken me from humble beginnings to the Himalayas and the Camino de Santiago. These events led me to write in the context of a diary and the spiritual experiences which interlock various countries, cultures, people, history and past life experiences. These experiences have shown me that life is a Camino filled with angels. That's why they all need to be acknowledged for their presence, giving encouragement to all who wish to take the first step on their Camino.

'Travelling the Camino, we start off as tourists and end up as pilgrims. That's my experience and I have covered many, all leading me to spiritual entities that amazed and enlightened my soul, making me long for more.'

— ELIZABETH McKENNA

CHAPTER ONE

Back on the Camino

God, my feet hurt! I'd been walking for five hours, which isn't a long time on the Camino, where you could be on the road all day and still want more. I was keeping a promise I had made: to go slow and smell the roses. As I sat on a bench watching my friend Trish shield her face from the sun and smile while butterflies danced in front of her, I thought about the notion of life being a journey and not a destination. It's a familiar concept, but it becomes real and tangible on the Camino. I wondered if, like the Camino, our destinations are set before we even pack our bags. This being her first Camino, Trish was mesmerised at the scale of the walk and all the help we were getting en route without even looking for it. There were hundreds of pilgrims from around the world, all intent on reaching Santiago de Compostela.

The road became quiet, and my mind began to drift. I inspected my feet. They looked alright, and yet, when I walked, my soles felt as though there were spikes coming out of them, sinking into the ground like the roots of a tree.

'Perhaps I am going to be locked to the ground and sprout wings?' I said to a little bird chirping away on the branch of a giant tree. I suppose I was a bit fearful that I wouldn't be able to keep going on this road or reach the next accommodation. The road and the pace would be dictated and the final destination would be announced as we made our way down the path, of that I was sure – just like the other roads on the other Caminos.

A youngish woman with a slow steady step approached us. She tossed her sun-bleached hair back from her face while her eyes remained fixed on a little brown terrier beside her. He was scurrying from side to side, shuffling his nose along the sandy path, oblivious to anyone around him.

'Did you bring him with you?' I asked.

'No, he must live locally, but he has been keeping me company,' she replied. 'What's wrong with your feet?' she added.

I didn't even realise I was rubbing them vigorously. 'I don't know,' I replied. 'I think it's the road trying to send me a message. It has the ability to make us stop wherever it chooses. It's happened before and if you don't listen, there will be a lot of struggles en route.'

'Have you been here before?' she asked.

'I have, but not on this particular route. A lot of roads lead to Santiago, and they are all powerful. Some people refer to them as the Holy Roads, others the Roman Roads. Regardless of what way you interpret them, they are full of mystery, history and presence of past generations. If you believe in spirits you will be intrigued; they make their presence known in the strangest of ways. I have learned that our loved ones are never far away; they are merely watching from behind the mirror, you won't be disappointed.'

'Do you believe that?' she asked and sat down beside us.

A familiar feeling swept over me: I knew we were meant to meet and that we would have a meaningful conversation.

'I do indeed,' I replied. I put my feet on the ground, but it was hot and gave no comfort so I slipped back on my socks and boots. 'I have felt its power and been led in circles and ended up in places I had no intention of going, and I've met people that helped me find my way.' I pointed to the large trees surrounding us, standing proud, waving their arms in the gentle breeze, their roots going back to the time of the Roman soldiers. 'If the trees could talk they could tell a tale or two,' I said, and we all laughed and sighed in agreement.

Claudia was a doctor from New York. She had come to Spain for a conference and then decided to walk the Camino. 'What made you come back on the Camino?' asked Claudia.

'You could say it was predicted from another level, like it was part of the plan for me,' I replied.

When she gave me an inquiring look, I told her about the promise I made to my dear friend Vinney the last time I saw him in 2014. We had been sitting in a café near Dublin Castle pretending all was good with our lives, but it wasn't – not for either of us. We were hurting, as both of us had just buried loved ones unexpectedly and were still suffering the shock that death leaves behind. In the space of a few months he had lost his beloved wife and his mother, and I had lost my brother and a very special aunt whom I loved dearly. When death comes, as it will, it rocks the soul. It leaves a crack in the heart and I don't believe it ever closes fully. I had never seen such a strong high-spirited man look so broken.

When I hugged him tight, he said, 'You believe in the angels, don't you, Liz?'

I reassured him that I did, that if it weren't for angels I probably wouldn't even have been there with him. They have always guided and looked after me ever since I can remember. I counselled him to ask them for help and not be afraid to tell them how sad he was feeling. They understand our heartache. I explained that there are so many angels around us, with us, at all times. Our guardian angel is forever with us. There is one angel that has always been close to me even in the darkest days and nights: Archangel Michael – God's right-hand man, one would say his personal secretary. He carries all our needs and fears to God, gives us reassurance and turns up in many forms. I told my friend to ask him for help and to also remember that our loved ones are close by, also ready to be called upon. I have had encounters with mine as far back as I can remember, even though I can't see them.

Vinney told me he had pains in his chest at night that took his breath away, and I advised him to see a doctor because the stress of mourning can cause our heart to be damaged physically and emotionally. He was so lonely I told him a prayer I always say to St Michael and I reassured him it always helped me:

St Michael the Archangel, guide me with your light, wrap me with your cloak of blue, protect me with your sword, and shield and love me with your heart.

'You need to slow up and recover from the shock that death brings,' I warned him. 'No more racing to the finish line, or hundreds of miles in one go. You've done that and seen the world and you haven't seen the Camino yet. We could go on the Camino, take our time, walk the Holy Road and smell the roses together. This way we will be close to all our departed loved ones,' I said.

'Alleluia,' he replied, hugging me with his big strong arms, and I saw a bit of the old spirit return as he put his hands in the air and said, 'Onwards and upwards.' They were the words he used when he was on a mission.

But it wasn't to be. Sadly, it was all too much for him. The crack in his heart was too big. It couldn't heal and he went to his beloved. I could hardly believe it, and neither could his family. Sometimes the call from our departed is stronger than the responsibility we feel towards those left behind.

'My friend Vinney picked this road, Claudia, and he is the one dictating where I stop and I'm not sure why. But I feel him with me every step of the way since before I left home.'

'How do you mean?' Claudia asked, looking confused.

'Well, he came to me in a dream when I was trying to make up my mind which route to take. I had planned and researched the Portuguese route, but he said Sarria. I woke up, wet with tears, saying the word Sarria. It was so real; he was like his old self and he was directing me. I rang our friend and asked her where this was. I was thinking he wanted me to go to Syria and was none too impressed, what with all the trouble and the catastrophe there. She told me it was part of the Camino's traditional route, which was a relief. He had been the leader on a few long cycling journeys and he is still leading the way here. Making sure I don't overdo it.'

I stood up, waved to other walkers and wished them 'Buen Camino'. Claudia, Trish and I then decided to book into a very smart hotel that once was a medieval building. I smiled at the abundance of roses all along the drive, and when I opened the front door, the corridor was also full of roses. He had certainly picked the right place for us to stay. I laughed out loud and marvelled at the coincidence – if there is any such thing. Is it just steps in life that are prepared for us, if we so wish to climb them, as Trish believed? We threw ourselves onto the beds to embrace a much-needed siesta. I marvelled at the fact that my feet were now strangely cool and pain free.

Later that evening as I was clearing the table for the food Claudia asked if she could record me talking about the Camino. I was surprised at her request but she explained that she didn't want to forget those she met. She was fiddling with her phone, trying to turn on the record button. Hunger was distracting me, and the smell of fresh salad and fish made my mouth water. I was thinking out loud, and I said, 'Some people will get over a death quite easily and see it as part of living, while others will mourn for eternity. Don't you agree?'

She nodded her head in agreement and indicated that she was recording. I decided to go with it.

'My friend Vinney spoke powerfully at his wife's funeral. I wish I'd recorded him. He sent a message to all men that day, from the heart. He always spoke of his wife as his "beloved". I don't know any other person who speaks that way about their wife. I can still see him standing on the pulpit addressing the few thousand people that loved and knew her in some capacity. The children were exemplary in putting the funeral together: speaking, singing and playing music while their hearts were broken. He told the men to love their wives and told everyone to love and mind their family. There was a roar like thunder circling that church. At first I thought it was a train, but there are no trains near that place and the sky was silent. I felt like he was giving a message straight from God himself.

'He was a man who read his bible and said grace before meals. When we were in Australia he would have a passage ready before the sun came up, and we would set out on the bikes for a long hard cycle. Vinney was actually keeping us safe; he was like our very own preacher reminding us to be careful. If you ever wanted a father figure, he would be the one you would choose.'

Later that night, in the bedroom, I thought about my friend, who was guiding me. Vinney was a true gentleman and had been like a father figure on so many of our trips. I thought of my own father and how he had dealt with my mother's passing and us children. It hadn't been easy.

'I forgot my sticks! I left them at the bench and I don't know how I will manage without them. And I forgot to pack my short light socks. I'll need an angel tomorrow,' I murmured to myself as I undressed in the room full of flowers that felt like home and smelled of roses.

'You can have mine. I can walk without them,' said Trish in her sleepy voice.

'Thank you, my angel!' It's funny, I was normally the one who passed out things to people, and this time I had to be humble and accept any help that came my way.

'You'll be alright, Liz,' Trish added, trying to tie down her bouncy, dark curls so she could plaster the night cream on her face. We had a

19

good hearty laugh and we said a prayer for everyone on the list that was growing by the day.

In the dark of the night I wondered why I was sent on this particular road. There is a question in every situation and I needed the answers. I felt the sensation of already knowing this road, the layout of the environment. This inexplicable sense of familiarity was not unknown to me. I smiled, curled up, thanked St Michael for his help and said a rosary to Our Lady.

CHAPTER TWO

Socks on the Camino

T he smell of toast and fresh coffee teased us as we stuffed our few belongings into the backpack. I had learned to carry very few belongings on the Camino, having sent items home on previous occasions. Trish had spent the morning looking for her socks only to find them wrapped around the blanket. When I put my bare feet into my open sandals they felt light, and I prayed they would stay that way all day.

Claudia arrived smiling, refreshed from her sleep. No one would think she was a doctor. It's hard to anticipate what people do for a living on the Camino; out of uniform we are all the same in old rugged shorts and T-shirts, displaying previous journeys and challenges. Some pilgrims carry a flag representing their hometowns and countries. I always feel at home in my old clothes. I could spend the entire summer in them and be extremely happy. When I was a child I never liked fancy clothes; it was too much bother trying to keep them clean.

Claudia handed me a package with a lovely pair of sky-blue socks. 'They are made especially for people with problems with their feet,' she said.

I could hardly believe it! 'You're an angel in disguise, an earth angel,' I said, admiring them.

She smiled and her whole face lit up. 'Do you believe in angels, Liz?'

'Indeed I do,' I said without hesitation. 'They have always been by my side. When I've been in a tricky situation and needing help, they have never let me down. They have saved my life many a time and always persist when they want to give me a message. Sometimes they slow me down to keep me safe. Do you believe?'

'I used to, when I was young, but now I just seek God's help,' she replied.

'You go straight to the top man then?'

'I guess so,' she said.

I looked up to the sun that was spreading over the sky – a hot day lay ahead. We caught up with the crowd of pilgrims and I wondered if they were all seeking God's help too.

'Are there any saints in your church in New York?' I asked. Some walkers passed by, almost knocking us over, such was their concentration. Their voices were raised as they said the rosary aloud. One girl in her twenties was limping like a lame dog. She was clearly in pain. My heart melted for her. Her beautiful brown eyes held a sadness that had nothing to do with her blisters.

'None. Only Jesus on the cross with white walls surrounding him. That's all that's in my church,' she replied.

'Ah, that paints a very sad picture in my mind,' I replied. A lonely figure flashed before me and I felt a deep sadness. I felt tears form and had to hold them back. 'Do you have a secretary?' I asked her.

'I do,' she said, surprised at my question.

'Do you not think you would have a lot of work and be tired out without one?'

She smiled and nodded.

'Well, do you not think God has the saints and angels to help lighten his burden? After all, they were here on this planet doing God's work tirelessly and some died in his name, including St James. St Michael is powerful and I would never leave a place without seeking his guidance, without making sure he knew I was on a mission. He has saved my life on many occasions.'

My feet were feeling fresh with the new socks and Trish – my other angel – had given me her sticks. She was motoring ahead chatting to anyone and everyone, happy as the day was long on her first Camino. She was praying for guidance and help with dealing with her mother who was elderly and terminally ill. She wanted to be brave and have the courage to be strong and help with the rest of the family with her mother's care. She loves the angels and the saints and, like me, is always happy with all the signs they leave her.

'Why did you go on the first Camino and where did you start from?' asked Claudia.

'It's a long strange story. I am pretty sure all the Caminos were planned without my knowledge. They must have been, just like our lives. I believe so much is planned and we have the power to follow the plan or to stay stuck in a moment in time and fail to move on and miss out on the fun. Do you know the history behind St James and the Camino roads?' I asked her.

'Only a morsel. I had heard about it, and as I was coming to the conference in Spain, I decided to see for myself.'

'I'll tell you what I know of the road and how I found out about it. It's hard to believe even for me.'

We adjusted the bags on our backs, sipped some water and synchronised our steps as we moved onward.

'Claudia, I have learned from my experience on previous Camino roads that it's the journey in between the posts that counts, and not the destination. What you can learn about yourself (the inner journey) can be challenging, sometimes terrifying, but at times it's so much fun, you want it to go on forever. That's why I believe life's journey is like a pathway on a Camino, and one way to find our purpose in life is to travel on a journey like this and see where we are led.'

'How did you come to that conclusion?' asked Claudia.

'Let me explain as best I can by showing you the way the journey started.'

CHAPTER THREE

St James and the Holy Road

My truth, my story, that I told Claudia that day as we walked in sync together is as follows:

I was introduced to St James by a psychic medium I encountered by chance. Her name was Margaret Solis, and she was from Glasgow in Scotland, where I was born and lived until I was a teenager. My sister told me about her and her great gift. I was curious and wanted to see for myself. Despite her being in high demand, I was lucky to avail of a very rare cancellation on one of the occasions I returned to Glasgow to visit my sister. Her house looked normal and she looked normal. When I sat down, she pulled out some cards and seemed to look through me. I was a bit unsure what to think.

She proceeded to tell me many things, including where I lived, how many children I had, what I worked at and the passion I had for solving a mystery that had consumed me since I was a child. This startled me and I was sure she was reading my mind. Then she became serious, stared at me and asked if I knew about St James and the Camino de Santiago. At the time I was engrossed in racing my bike, swimming in the sea, teaching people to swim and rearing my children, and I had no inclination to walk across mountains.

I told her I knew nothing about the Camino, but I had heard of St James being a disciple of Jesus. She continued to mention him and every time she spoke his name, chimes rang from behind her. She saw the look on my face and said, 'That's St James making his presence known.' I was a bit freaked out but pretended otherwise.

She smiled and asked me to mention her in my writings. I assured her I had no intention of going on the Camino, as I was going to cycle across Australia. She agreed that I would do that too, as well as climbing higher mountains and writing about these experiences. I was baffled. I only scribbled in a diary and wrote the odd letter. Even punctuation freaked me out, and I thought about my teachers giving out to me as a child because I didn't put dots in the right places. I laughed nervously. There was no way I was going to be writing. The chimes rang out once again and I began to sweat in the cool small room. She smiled and proceeded to tell me about my father, and the struggle I had acknowledging him when he paid me visits from the spirit world. She also mentioned 'smoke smells' that made me cough.

She went on to say the Camino was, for many, a form of spiritual retreat for their spiritual growth, and that my father was constantly with me and would be with me on the Camino. I laughed, because deep down I knew she was right; but I would not acknowledge his presence as my mother had always been my guide, and I did not want him taking her place. Margaret also said that, on the Camino we are walking in history, with generations of past warriors, and many people have acknowledged that the road had the ability to seek out their intuition, causing them to go round in circles, not only on the path but in their minds, and I would find out for myself just how powerful it could be.

Before I left, she told me to read Paulo Coelho's *The Pilgrimage* and Shirley MacLaine's *The Camino* to help me understand what was ahead of me. She was most insistent that I read *Same Soul Many Bodies* by Dr Brian Weiss and *Out on a Limb* by Shirley MacLaine. I left, lamenting how wrong she was about my future and how I'd just wasted good money and time.

I did cross Australia for my fortieth birthday challenge and that is when I got to know my friend Vinney. He was so funny in the mornings with his hair frizzled, his helmet bouncing on the handlebars, his back pockets bulging with his lunch and the sun rising behind him. We would line up beside him and say the prayers. He was our shepherd and he was asking for God's help to keep us safe on the road. In the evening he always had a piece of the bible ready and we said prayers of gratitude. That journey opened me up spiritually and physically and helped me build confidence in myself and to trust and acknowledge God in my life more openly. I have Vinney to thank for that, and the memory has lasted more than twenty years.

As I spoke so candidly to Claudia I could sense Vinney around me. Emotions filled me as we continued walking and admiring the roses hanging from walls and shooting up from every crevice in the ground.

Silence fell for a while, and Claudia asked quietly, 'So, did you climb higher mountains as Margaret predicted?'

I smiled and thought about my trip to the Himalayas, from Lhasa to Kathmandu, and how Vinney had enticed me to go there, despite my only having been to lower climbs in Australia, Vietnam and Scotland. Strange as this may seem, these journeys, exotic and difficult as they may seem, served in my preparation, both physically and spiritually, for the Camino de Santiago.

On reflection, these were Caminos in themselves. I perceived that all roads led to Santiago, but Santiago can be any place of spiritual worship: where one feels safe – even in the midst of a storm – surrounded by mountains in a strange country.

Claudia marvelled at what she termed 'achievements' but I was quick to tell her they had only been possible with the help of the angels and saints.

CHAPTER FOUR

We Are All on a Camino

I believe the Camino can be anywhere – not only in Santiago – and our angels are all around us, every minute of every day. We have to be able to read the signs; ask them for help and acknowledge this help with gratitude. The road to Santiago has taught me that we will meet people at various times in our lives for reasons unknown to us. Some will stay with us for a long time while others stay for only a passing moment. I saw Claudia as one of them, here to make my feet feel better, and for that she would be rewarded with a plenitude for her good deed.

During the Middle Ages, when people needed to rectify 'choices', some went on a pilgrimage seeking a plenitude indulgence: it's like forgiveness for deeds done. It was taking time to reflect on life and making changes when they returned. Some never made it back home because the roads were dangerous with no footpaths, no maps, very few places to stay and eat and just basic signs. People depended on others for their daily needs. Those that helped were kept in the prayers of the travellers, who, in turn, were earning plenitude indulgences. The Road of St James to Santiago de Compostela was one of the most important Christian pilgrimages to be travelled. When it is complete, you get your certificate and have completed your indulgence. It's like absolution while we are alive.

I have found that most people we meet on the Camino will give out positive encouragement and enlighten us. Yet, here, like everywhere else, there are negative people who are looking for something to go wrong; listening to them can make us fearful, like watching the news. I work with young people and they get frightened with all the wars. I try to tell them that God is in everything and nature will always churn up a storm, but to make sure to watch out for the rainbow afterwards. I tell them prayer helps when you are afraid, because sometimes the one you can't see feels safer and can be trusted better than the one you can see. We will all have our turn in life where we seek prayer from others and God's help. Some leave that until they are dying. Many people have asked me to pray for them when they don't pray themselves, or even believe in God. I had a friend who told me he did not believe in God and laughed when I would tell him stories of times I asked God for help. His wife was going through life-changing surgery and I believed her faith was being challenged, so I gave her an angel to take with her. When his wife was making a miraculous recovery, my friend said that he believed there must indeed be a place and someone greater than us, more powerful than us. He was quick to add, however, that he didn't believe in the Church. Considering the abuse controversies I could understand this, but I was so happy for him, for the sense of peace I could see coming from him.

We agreed that the church was simply a place to go and visit, like we visit family and friends. It was a choice. The clergy were God's workers, and, being human, were as susceptible to evil as we all are. The endemic abuse of the vulnerable has destabilised the Church as an organisation but not God's house. I love churches, any churches; religion is another thing.

I found God on the Holy Road: in the flowers, trees and wind, and in the humans we meet. Around you people are walking in unison towards a common destination, surrounded by beautiful scenery. Nobody wants to know where you come from and what your religion is, only that you are a comrade. It doesn't matter what you believe in on the Camino. There are people of varied cultures and beliefs, religion and no religion, all seeking the same thing: peace within themselves and in the world around them, and perhaps a soulmate!

Walking with Trish and Claudia helped me to open my mind, be more observant and listen to intuition as we trotted along each day, trying to make sense of what lay ahead. Every day started with a prayer for safety, and every night ended with another in gratitude. Claudia had been keen for me to tell her more about these angels and saints I was referring to. She asked if I had been writing down these stories and was aghast when I told her I was only keeping a simple diary. Trish echoed Claudia and pushed me into thinking about doing more. That night, in the accommodation, I had a lot to think about – these ladies were saying what Margaret Solis had said. Perhaps it was time I took it seriously, like I had promised the angels.

CHAPTER FIVE

Cycling with Mary

T he next morning we walked in blessed silence. I was grateful for that because my mind was filled with my friend Mary. The first time I stood on the Camino road I was unaware I was on it! I was on a cycle trip to Malaga with my friend Mary and an English lad, Jay, who asked if he could join us. He was grieving his father's death and I hadn't the heart to deny him the company. I did warn him about teaming up with two eccentrics, though. There we were, map-reading, seeking our road to Malaga and all around us were statues of St James and yellow arrows and shells pointing in the direction of Santiago de Compostela.

Mary always has a sparkle in her eye and a sense of adventure in her heart. She is adored by Val, her husband of over fifty years, and her children and grandchildren. We met while doing a Triathlon. We shared many things, including a love for the sea and a devotion to St Teresa of Avila. Mary lost her father when she was seven, and his death left a hollow in her heart, just like my mother's death left in mine. Mary bought a little house in Spain and ended up doing a degree in Spanish and Theology. There we were en route to Malaga via Santiago. It was my first time on the Camino and each day I found it hard to remember where we'd come from. I just followed my nose. The first time I was on the road I found it hard each day to remember where I had come from. In my effort to update my diary, every morning I would say, 'Mary, where were we yesterday?' She found it amusing that I could lead the way without a map and still have no idea of where we'd left from. Ever since I was a child, I've followed my instinct, acknowledging the help I get from my guardian angels.

In January 2008, Mary and I set out to follow St Teresa's footsteps and see some of her convents, starting in Malaga, moving onwards to Seville, Córdoba and Granada and back to Malaga. That journey unwound so many things in my life and uprooted memories that I did not know were hidden in my memory box, some for a very long time.

Mary and I were having breakfast that first morning, with one eye nervously on a large grey cloud looming in the distance. I remember Mary making her way to the counter to get more coffee, sliding in the cycling shoes. She looked so funny. We mounted our bikes, blessed ourselves and headed in the direction of Seville. It was a hard climb up to the mountain pass, especially with the wind howling through our helmets. Malaga's history spans about 2,800 years, making it one of the oldest cities in the world. Being anywhere in the province of Malaga makes you feel firmly planted in the past. I felt connected to its past and that strange sensation of 'knowing' the road, despite never having been on it. At night I dreamed of places that we would encounter the next day.

It was there that I overheard men talk about Santiago. They were doing part of the Camino with the intention of finishing it in the summer. I didn't realise Santiago was on that route. I knew of the French route, but was oblivious about all the others. A quick check of the map informed me the roads leading to Santiago included one from Malaga. I hadn't been cycling in the mountains since Nepal with Vinney two years previously. I figured this cycle would be a doddle compared to that, though one old man we encountered thought we were insane cycling in the mountains in January. But Mary and I had our angels. Within a few minutes of meeting that old man a butterfly flew by me – a rare sight in January. This was the first sign of St Teresa. The mountains soared around us and it reminded me of the time I hit the summit in Scotland in the Cairngorm Mountains and thought I was in heaven. It's the elation of the challenge and the magic of watching the world from a height.

We freewheeled into the town at speed and we squealed in delight. Sometimes a sense of danger can bring excitement, but we weren't afraid, as we believed we were being watched from above. When you sense the spirits in the breeze surrounding you, it is reassuring. Our descent ended at a picture of the Sacred Heart of Jesus on the wall of an old twelfth-century church. Oh, how I love him, the most beautiful heart ever to beat. I couldn't take my eyes off him. We parked the bikes and walked inside to find a funeral Mass starting. As I knelt to pray I could feel an overwhelming feeling of joy and gratitude in my heart, and I thought I would cry. But I learned how to hold back tears when I was young, even in a special moment. Instead I listened to my heartbeat and thanked God for the gift.

It's amazing how we could relax and enjoy the cycle without the heavy traffic. It's like living with a clear unfearful mind, smelling the roses while living in harmony with nature. We were like two kids running free, milling down the road with hardly a breeze. Once we were stopped at the side of the road, drinking water and eating cheese from our back pockets, when a motorbike pulled up beside us. A young man dismounted and asked if we were okay. We assured him we were but inquired what the best road to Seville was. He pointed to a completely different road to the one we had thought. Peace could have been short-lived had we not met him. He was our angel; St Michael was working his magic.

We eventually stopped at a hotel only to find ourselves amidst great joy and excitement as children were celebrating Little Christmas. Sweets were raining down on them from the floats of the parade. We put the bikes up against the walls and joined in the fun. I don't know what people were shouting, but every time they did they got missiles with sweets of all kinds. Sweets were landing in front of us and we were like kids, gathering them up and filling our pockets. Some hit me on the head and I realised I still had my helmet on. I whipped it off and used it to hold my bounty. Mary and I were a sight, sitting on the side of the road munching the sweets and storing what was left for later emergencies. The owner of the hotel was standing with a crowd of other people, and when I looked up they were breaking their sides laughing at us. I was glad we drew the line at not battling the kids for the toys that had been thrown from on high.

The excitement and the sugar rush left me tired but wide awake most of the night. I remember saying to Mary that I had considered going head to head with a young girl over a doll. I was laughing, but Mary replied quietly, 'I never liked dolls.' I thought that odd, as I had loved them. As sleep eluded me, I tried to meditate to quieten my mind. At night, fear of the unknown can creep into the mind, like ivy creeps up in unexpected places. My mind was uprooting all sorts of dormant memories from childhood. When another child brutalised my beautiful doll with wavy hair and a spotted dress, I was devastated. I hated my father when he thought I was overreacting. 'It's just a doll,' he had said, completely oblivious to the fact that aside from my brother, that doll was the only thing I felt I had left to love. I prayed to St Teresa:

'Let nothing disturb you, let nothing trouble you. All things pass, everything changes, except God.'

Mary and I loved cathedrals, so when we arrived in Seville, the cathedral of San Pedro was our first stop. It is one of the largest Gothic cathedrals in Europe and the third largest after St Peter's Basilica in Rome, and St Paul's in London. Sometimes in cathedrals you can sense past lives calling out for recognition; sometimes it's very clear, other times it comes from within.

Walking along the lighted Moorish area and the Jewish streets was deeply affecting. I met a young man from Rome who told me he had regular dreams about experiences he could not have possibly had in this lifetime. He said walking up the streets in Seville left him feeling like he was walking in familiar territory, and yet this was his first time there. I had the same feeling, I told him. Standing in an environment like the ancient Alcázar, you could feel your body reacting to that century, like a deep-seated memory had come alive and wanted to be acknowledged.

I was questioning which cultures my body was recognising and how many times I had been around in previous lives! The amount of people that are 'just curious' or 'fixated' with looking back in history makes me wonder are they also seeking answers to something they can't explain that pops up in their dreams and thoughts. I wondered could we learn from the past lives and possibly remember events from the past by staying in places long enough to stir the subconscious. Amidst these streets I felt I should be walking on tip-toe so as not to disturb the dead. Perhaps it was having a revelation of a past life memory. I read about reliving past lives through the psychic memory; this type of memory gives us hope that life is everlasting and we come back many times in different bodies. When cycling through a foreign land, the mind becomes open and awareness increases. Perhaps not being familiar with the language and being aware of danger, which could strike any time, we learn to rely more on our other senses. Awareness becomes second nature and intuition takes over the mind, every experience is elated and lived with gratitude for every moment, for one never knows when the last one will come.

The following day we followed in the footsteps of Santa Teresa de Avila in the heart of the Santa Cruz neighbourhood of Seville. When Teresa was fourteen her mother died and she asked Our Lady to be her mother. This information intrigued me, as Mary lost her father when she was six and I lost my mother when I was two. Though centuries apart, we all had an early loss in common. We arrived at the impressive wooden door to her convent, which houses the only known portrait of Teresa painted during her lifetime as well as the original manuscript of her best-known work, Las Moradas, the Dwellings of the Interior Castle, in which she speaks about the struggle of the butterfly and the soul.

Our visit to the Casa de Pilatos, a residence dating back to the fourteenth century, left me feeling very unsettled. We were standing at a large Roman statue, listening to the interpreter, when all of a sudden my body became as cold as ice. I touched Mary's hand and she jumped.

'You are stone cold like the statue,' she said.

I was shivering and my heart was racing. 'I feel strange, Mary, like I've been here before, and I think I'm dying,' I said.

It was amazing the feelings I had in there. That experience reminded me of when I was a child tucked up in bed sound asleep only to be woken up by something and feel my feet and legs stiff, frozen. My heart would be pounding and I felt the Holy Spirit was forewarning me of something. I felt I had died in those dreams and when I told my granny, she would always comfort me and say, 'That's okay, Elizabeth. I often had them too, old souls, that's all we are.' Then we would laugh and she would pour a cup of tea, and I would wish I could stay in her house forever.

I was tired the morning we were heading to Alcalá Del Río. Our back pockets were bursting with fruit and bread for the lunch as we said goodbye to our hosts. They wished us a 'Buen Camino' and I got excited at the thoughts of St James. But St Teresa was the one we were following. I reminded myself I would someday reach Santiago de Compostela, but for now was on a different Camino. We faced a tough climb that morning. After twenty kilometres the descent began fast and furious. The golden trees on both sides went by like a tornado, and it was hard to see anything other than the front wheel spinning. Prayers and promises to St Michael and to my mother were in full force. Without stopping for breath, we began to climb once again. Despite it being January, I was very warm and yearned to discard some clothing. When we arrived at the top of the mountain I wasn't long pulling off my coat.

Our faces were red and our hair was standing on end when we pulled off our helmets. Steam literally rose from our bodies. Mary, Jay and I stood, admiring the view and savouring the sense of satisfaction we felt as we saw the mountain valley behind us and realised how far we'd come. There was a silence in the mountains that day. I never even heard a bird sing. I guess they were watching us and waiting for lunch!

As we entered Alcalá Del Río via the old Roman bridge, I said to Mary that a sense of familiarity was filling me yet again. I felt that people were waiting for us to arrive. We headed into the hostel utterly exhausted. My whole body was crying out for mercy; every sinew was on fire. Following a hot shower and some rest, we headed out to explore. Soon we were staring at a castle on a hilltop; it radiated history and mystery. It's hard to explain the sensation I felt when interacting with the people in the street. They nodded to us as if they knew us; it felt like we belonged there, had gone away and were now being welcomed home.

We sat in a lovely traditional restaurant with brightly tiled floors and colourful tablecloths. With tired eyes we looked at the map, contemplating the next day's cycle. The map showed an enormous climb ahead and I felt we needed to be prepared. There was something niggling at me and I couldn't put my finger on it, but it was persistent and I felt something was waiting in the background and time would tell what it was. I suggested to Mary that we go to the church to let them know we had arrived safely and to ask for more help the next day. We all laughed, but I was deadly serious – it's not a good idea to ask for more help without acknowledging in gratitude the help you have already been given.

The altar in the Church of the Annunciation was beautiful. Our Lady was depicted with the Angel Gabriel on one side of her and St Michael on the other. Beautiful yellow, pink and white flowers, a perfect tribute to the Queen of Heaven, adorned the altar, which prompted me to hum, 'Oh Mary we crown thee with blossoms today, Queen of the Angels and Queen of the May.' My heart sang as it always does with those words, something so innate and loving always hits me and I closed my eyes while standing at her feet. I felt she was standing right beside me and St Michael was protecting me too. Such was the love that filled my heart, I shed a tear.

Jay wandered around looking at the statues and he said to me, 'Liz, if I was to pick a religion it would be Catholic.' He loved our churches. He wasn't brought up with religion; he was left to make up his own mind. I'm not sure I could have got through a day in my life without God to talk to. I would have been totally lost, or even dead, of that I'm sure.

We walked outside to find the moon's brightness had lit up the whole town, making every blade of grass visible. Under its extraordinary light, the ancient details of the buildings and statues were illuminated. We could hear the water flowing under the bridge. It was a cleansing river; it washed away all negativity, which was why, I believe, this place was so peaceful and everything seemed to move so slowly. I felt pure serenity in that place. God was present in that town and in its people.

CHAPTER SIX

Following the Footsteps of St Teresa de Avila

It may seem strange to you to be walking one Camino while thinking of another, but it's not. The Camino is life, and we regularly go about our day or week pondering on things past, people and places that have brought us to where we are. My first Camino, cycling with Mary and Jay, was a pivotal trip during my life, one that brings great joy and comfort to remember. Without following the footsteps of St Teresa, I would never have followed those of St James.

After another blissful day of cycling, we crossed another Roman bridge to enter Córdoba. As was our wont, we went straight to the Church of Santiago. Access to the church is made through a segmental arch, decorated with scallop shells, a symbol of the Camino de Santiago; people wear the scallop shells around their neck or attach them to their backpacks while they follow the signs (also in the form of scallop shells) to Santiago de Compostela. The three church bells rang as we entered and I immediately remembered Margaret Solis telling me that St James made his presence known to me through the sound of his bells.

We lit candles for all who walk the Camino and may be in need of help from St Michael, including ourselves, because travelling into the unknown brings great challenges. There were no other visitors in the church, just us, and I was glad. From the time I was seven years old I would go by myself to church and just sit there and look at the statues around me. I wanted to know their names. We were anxious to visit the church of San Miguel (St Michael) also, and it was worth it. As we approached its beautiful rose window above the entrance my heart beat loudly and I felt the Holy Spirit saying, 'He is all around.' This was a special church for those with devotion to St Michael.

After a decent sleep in a lovely hostel, we awoke to a blanket of thick fog hanging low over the town – not a pretty sight for those contemplating cycling into the mountains towards Granada. Perhaps that was what had been niggling at me in the church; perhaps we were given a warning to be careful. We took our time with breakfast and met a group of young people in their twenties, who told us about the fine skiing to be had near Granada. This excited both Jay and Mary. The fog was distracting me; it reminded me of the time a dense fog came in from the sea while I was in the Mull of Kintyre in Scotland. Visibility was zero and we were urged to stand completely still until it lifted. With that thought in mind, I said to Mary that we should wait until the fog lifted before we left.

It was taking its time. I was happy to wait and read a book in the little café, but Mary was anxious to go in case it took too long to get to Granada. I knew she was thinking of the skiing and getting excited. She is the only person I know that can switch her mind from one thing to another in an instant and get excited about the next adventure. I'm different; I prefer to savour the moment and don't like to think too far ahead. Eventually we relented. We put on our vests with the flashing lights, lit up the bikes on the back and front, and put on armbands and our bright clothes. I still couldn't see very much and I worried whether traffic would be able to see us.

At 11 a.m. we moved out nervously into the main road. I was feeling incredibly uneasy and the song 'Mull of Kintyre' kept rattling around my head, like a warning, so I prayed to St Michael. As we climbed, the fog worsened. I was in front, on a bend with such a steep incline I was forced to get out of my saddle and push the bike. I felt I was going against my instincts, which were telling me to keep still until it was safe. I didn't. I was not trusting my gut and I feared the consequences.

The next bend gave us all a fright. On our left was a large bus with a trail of cars behind it. There were police on motorbikes and we could hear an ambulance coming in the distance behind us. There was a body on the road and a motorbike lying on its side with the engine humming. A policeman was covering up the body. It seemed that despite reflective clothing, this poor motorcyclist had been hit by the bus. This shook us and we wanted to leave the road. Thankfully, there was a narrow lane nearby and we scurried into it to wait for the fog to lift. I thanked St Michael for guiding us and prayed for the family of the person who had so tragically died. I could see Jay was shook; he had gone pale and quiet. I felt responsible for him – he was after all taking our advice. Mary was quiet – I think the excitement she had felt about the skiing and in Granada and the convent of St Teresa slipped her mind.

Eventually the fog lifted and we faced into a very tough climb. The mountains seemed to mock me, saying, 'Are you giving up? Do we win?' At times like these I pray to my friend Ann and say, 'Give us a push, Ann. You know how hard it can be.' Suddenly, the downhill started out of the blue with no signs to warn us; we went down and around the Sierra Nevada Mountains like spinning tops, fast and furious. There was snow on one side and the sun belting down on the other, which made it scary. The sun was shining in our eyes and the road was so narrow coming up to meet us. I was grateful for the sunglasses for I knew one blink and we could be part of the history on the Roman Roads. There was a lot to be thankful for in that downhill, mostly the fact that there was very little traffic. Every day on the bike is a new adventure. It is filled with people going about their business, and among them are the saints and earth angels just waiting to help; they are part of the environment and are still fulfilling their duties as God's helpers.

We were following in the footsteps of St Teresa, so as soon as we entered Granada we headed to the monastery of San José de Granada, which was the sixteenth and penultimate convent to be founded by St Teresa. St John of the Cross, a devoted friend of St Teresa, was sent to Avila to bring her to Granada and set up the Carmelite Order. But St Teresa was ill and was busy preparing the foundation in Burgos, which was the last place she was to complete herself. As she was unable to come in person, she appointed as founder and prioress M. Ana de Jesús (Lobera) who was nicknamed 'the captain of the prioresses' and to whom St John of the Cross was to later dedicate his Spiritual Canticle when they were both in Granada. She also chose the other sisters who were to start the life of the female Barefoot Carmelite Order in Granada. The founders arrived in Granada on 20 January 1582 when the life of that monastery began and it has not been interrupted since. St Teresa is all around Granada. One can see her in the faces of the nuns that silently go about their business.

Granada is similar to Avila, the walled city where St Teresa was born. For years she travelled throughout Spain, establishing the Carmelite Order in many cities. Her legacy and that of St John of the Cross and of Our Lady of Mount Carmel is embedded and entwined in the foundations of Spain and in the atmosphere of all the Holy Roads and Caminos. Granada has a history of many religions co-existing. I lamented at the lack of that today. Each person houses the Holy Spirit in the form of a heartbeat, regardless of religion.

We woke up the following day at six o'clock. It was 20 January, the anniversary of the founding of St Teresa's convent in Granada. A special Mass was said as her statue, dressed in beautiful flowers, was paraded in homage. We were overjoyed and gratified at being in Granada for such a special day in the Carmelite calendar.

Neither Mary nor Jay had forgotten about the chance to ski. I was up for the challenge but still prayed like mad to St Michael to keep us safe. We gathered what we needed for the day trip and caught the bus to the slopes. The bus journey was spectacular; high snow-capped mountains bathing in the sun were awe-inspiring. It was a long way up and our ears were popping with the altitude. It reminded me of the Himalayas. When we arrived at the slopes, we saw children and toddlers having the time of their lives. Surely I was up for it. We queued for boots and skis. Jay was ready first and moved out confidently, with a look of delight on his face. When I ventured out, I slipped immediately and the man caught me. Then he took the time to show us how to move and stop. He kept telling Mary that she needed pantaloons. It was then I noticed that Mary was wearing only a pair of tights. She had no idea and accused the man of taking her trousers while she was trying on the skis. He was denying it strenuously and I couldn't stop laughing; the whole thing, the confusion, the tights, it was like a pantomime. Eventually she got sorted and we laughed till we nearly got sick on our way to the ski lift.

After we jumped off, we moved forward at great speed while holding hands. We couldn't stop. A young man, who was to be our instructor, grabbed us and we clung tight. I was swaying one way and Mary the other and he was just standing looking at us. He certainly earned his wages that day. He placed us in the beginners' section and we made some progress, all while children were zooming up and down around us. Mary suddenly worried about breaking her legs, which for some reason made me laugh too. No sooner had she said it, a very large white and red butterfly with a spot of yellow landed at my feet and sat at my right-hand side.

'Mary, look, we don't have to worry. An angel sent from St Teresa just to reassure us we are being led and minded.'

Oh the joy to see that butterfly in the midst of the mountains in January. It filled me with love and I felt sad for those without the comfort of God or the angels; without such comfort, worry must be overwhelming. We had a great time enjoying the snow – sliding, falling and laughing like two kids. No matter what age you are life should be fun, and we should always remember that God gave us the ability to be joyful. I wondered why so many dwelt on the sad when joy was so much more rewarding. Exhausted and exhilarated we sat and watched the children. Sipping a mineral, I contemplated nature at its best and thanked St Teresa for acknowledging us for following in her footsteps – that day was our reward! Every time I think of Mary in her tights wondering what happened to her trousers, I laugh out loud. That anniversary day of the founding of St Teresa's monastery in Granada will always be fondly remembered.

With a mixture of sadness and jubilation, we prepared for the last day of cycling from Granada to Malaga. The heavy bags hanging off our bikes looked like large elephant ears. Finding our way out of the city was difficult. I turned to my angels. They answered through a young man who came along and showed us the road out. The road became undulating with spurts of climbing that lasted a couple of hours. We stopped and looked at the map and realised we were in the midst of the mountains; somehow we'd missed the turn for the low road to Malaga and we landed in the mountains climbing again. We decided to just keep going. No one ever goes back on the Camino; they just find a new route – learn from mistakes and move on. There was nothing around us but huge steeples of grey rock and our food supplies were dangerously low, so when we saw a shop called Naranja, which means orange in Spanish, the relief was palpable. It was surrounded by oranges and lemons, on the trees and hanging from the doors and walls – an oasis amidst the rocky wilderness. A cheerful young couple in the thirties welcomed us, and the smell of good food and the fruit was intoxicating. As we awaited our order outside, the young man brought us out some freshly squeezed orange juice. A group of six racing cyclists on their Sunday cycle landed, and as cyclists are inquisitive by nature, it wasn't long before conversation began. Jay was delighted to tell them how far we had come. One lad asked about the bags and the weight we were carrying and told us about the road we were on, pointing upwards towards the highest point that twisted around a bend shading the other side of the mountain. He advised us to go back. We smiled and said we had climbed this far and would keep going. They left as quickly as they'd come and disappeared in line like a flock of geese.

Heading out again with tired legs we began to climb; the food had given us energy and our back pockets were now full of food in case we became stranded. Those mountains are called the El Chaparral because they are similar to the ones in America used for cowboy films. It was a clear day and the views were spectacular – snow on one side and the sun on the other. I thanked God for sending us there, and acknowledged the hardest point in any of life's challenges is getting over the hurdles and persevering to the end. Fear of failing denies the struggle and the satisfaction and joy that wait at the end of a challenge. The descent was tricky and scary; we must have been doing fifty miles an hour. At that speed, all one can do is pray and hope for the best. The bags were shaking, sweat was running down our faces and my hands were numb from holding on so tight. I knew if one of us slipped, we were all gone over the cliff and down in a heap at the bottom of the mountain.

After a long struggle we arrived on the coast road of Malaga. I was delighted to see the ocean. The breeze and the smell enhanced my senses and all tiredness was forgotten in an instant. We found a bed and breakfast in Malaga. After the man kindly allowed us to put the bikes in the hallway and he was stamping our passports, something strange happened. I felt I was looking at him through glass, and he seemed to look strange, a different person. I felt I had seen him before and I was catapulted back in time. Jay felt something similar, and I was uncomfortable leaving the passports with him. This feeling of familiarity only deepened as we went to our bedrooms. Jay asked to be moved to a different room because he said there was a creepy feeling about the first one.

Exhaustion ensured I feel asleep immediately, but I knew it, I was transported via a visualisation of what I can only describe as a past life experience. I was in a large building surrounded by pillars, dressed in an old-fashioned flowing dress and a hat. A man with a chisel and hammer was in the room. I recognised him as my husband. I heard a noise from behind a large door. When I opened it I saw soldiers wearing sack-like clothes trying to invade the house. I closed the door, opened another and was faced with a large bear or Alsatian. I screamed at a young boy in the corner not to run. This boy had appeared in a dream the night before; we had been in a boat on the ocean together. As the soldiers reached me and picked me up, my screams joined those of the other people outside. I awoke with a start, stood up and promptly fell over Mary's bed. I'd pins and needles and my feet felt dead. Mary was sitting up looking up above the window, where there seemed to be the shape of a dove on the wall. It seemed the Holy Spirit filled the room and we prayed together. I shivered with the cold as I recounted my dream to Mary. We asked St Teresa to come and dispel all disturbances.

Experiences like this have me totally believing in past lives and the unconscious mind being instilled in us as a memory waiting to unfold; perhaps there was unfinished business to attend to. In the morning, Jay came in and he looked shook up and tired. He too had experienced a bad dream. We went down to have coffee out in the street café, and I felt funny, like I hadn't woken up and was still looking through glass. Needless to say, it was unsettling when I heard that Jay had dreamt of a young boy in a big house running away from a large animal. In his dream the young boy had reluctantly killed the animal with a pitchfork because he couldn't escape it. I was relieved. I wondered if we were rekindling something unfinished in a past life that had been haunting us. That night Jay also dreamt about his dad for the first time; he was in the garden and had found God.

The day unfolded and we went about enjoying the sea and the city, as if nothing unusual had happened. We visited the fifteenth-century cathedral and I wondered if my dream had taken place in the same century, as St Teresa and St John of the Cross had been born then too. They had been prominent throughout our journey through various signs, most especially the butterfly in the snow. St Teresa tells us that all we need is already inside us, like the lamp waiting to be rubbed clear to bring out the beauty of each individual. We all need to keep positive and keep the lamp lit inside by meditation and always being thankful for the day; that's what I think is important: living each moment and not wasting them. Leaving the cathedral, I felt a beautiful feeling run through me and heard voices sing out from every corner. I 'netted' this feeling in my memory to unwind at will whenever the need arose. It was a safe and loving feeling which is hard to describe. I felt God rejoicing and there was a sense of mystery about. There was something in the air waiting to unfold, and I would watch out for it. We spent a very different second night at that bed and breakfast. The man seemed different, kind and helpful, and we all slept well. It was a weird experience all the same.

Things got hairy on the road to the airport. Unforeseen road works forced us into a very dangerous situation on a motorway near the largest roundabout I have ever seen in my life. We tried in vain to find someone to give us a lift to the airport. Panic was setting in and I turned to St Michael. Just then two men in a large white transit van arrived, and I knew help was here. I was right.

We all have lessons to learn in life and on that particular trip, my lesson was to trust in God for everything, and to listen and watch for the answer to questions I constantly ask. I realised that if we ask God and the angels for help, we will receive help, in the form of what is best for us, what will help us with our purpose in life, in particular the stage in life we are at. This is the reason we should always ask for what is for our benefit and our good and for the good of others when seeking help from the angels. Faith and trust beats running around like a headless chicken, fearing the worst with an over-active imagination. St Teresa teaches us that when we have God, we have everything.

CHAPTER SEVEN

Back on the Camino of Roses

Here I was finally en route to Santiago de Compostela, following the road of St James with help from the yellow signs and arrows. Claudia, Trish and I walked until six o'clock that evening, when we came upon a building that I knew was the place we had to stop: the walls were decorated with roses and a painted sign outside read, 'Free Hugs' in various languages. Volunteers greeted us with refreshments. There was a map of the world on the wall and everyone signing the book placed a pin beside their hometown. I was intrigued with the environment and asked if they had accommodation. To my delight, a beautiful lady with the darkest of eyes illuminating great love said there was, and it was free and included dinner and breakfast. I found out later it was opened by an Irish man who had been living in America. He walked the Camino, found his dream, fundraised and returned to open a place to help pilgrims.

I had seen 1999 written up twice that day, and I began to ponder on the date. I was reminded of my brother-in-law. He died in 1999 and on a previous trip I had dreamt of him and here he was again: he wanted recognition. Trish and Claudia noticed that I had gone quiet, so I told them why and how this wasn't the first time my brother-in-law had made himself known. The night he took ill in 1999, my deceased mother-in-law visited me in a dream. She was carrying a young boy with blonde hair and she asked me to look after him. When I woke up I asked my husband who in his family had blonde hair when they were young. He told me his brother Jack was fair. I told him about his mother visiting me and I felt there was something wrong with Jack. My husband was used to my weird dreams and me waking up screaming and shouting. He never paid much attention to them and this was no exception.

The call came that same morning. My sister-in-law rang to say that Jack was being admitted to hospital. That's what my mother-in-law wanted: there were no other family members living in Dublin, only us, so I had to go there immediately. I rang my husband and left a message. The doctor was leaving when I arrived in Jack's room. He had just been told he had a terminal tumour in his stomach and liver. I was as shocked as he was; we were both unsure what to say. I went over and hugged him, and said he would be OK. He thanked me and said he wouldn't. He just wanted to live to see his daughter's baby born. Kate, his daughter, was pregnant with his first grandchild and it was due in six months. I said he would live to see the child, and longer. His will to live was strong, and God granted his wish. I felt he was with me on the cycle and again on the Camino telling me to keep in touch with the family, and he wanted me to write this to reassure other people that they are never alone, not even on the highest mountain or in a lonely bed.

'God, you are lucky to have such faith and understanding of the Camino,' said Trish.

Claudia nodded in agreement and added, 'Yes, and you're lucky to have such faith in angels too.'

I assured them that it wasn't easy to come to terms with the messages or with the experiences they ignited, but they presented things that needed attending to, and that was that. I felt at peace with them, as we sat together in the garden smelling the roses. After washing our clothes in an old stone basin, we settled down with the other pilgrims of varied nationalities to a generous feast. We all spoke about why we were on the Camino. Regardless of where we are from, people share similar wants and needs, and I felt blessed and happy to be sitting around that table. I even forgot about my sore feet.

A Spanish man of seventy asked us all why we were there and if we had walked the Camino before. He had no English and needed an interpreter, so we spoke slowly as we shared our motivations. I told him about my friend Vinney, that I had been there before and I felt my soul was calling me back. After Trish spoke about her purpose, Maria, a lovely lady in her fifties from South America, told us about the death of her husband and how she still mourned for him after three years. We talked and walked outside while watching the butterflies dance around us. I told Maria about Santa Teresa of Avila and how she spoke about breaking free from struggles and likened it to the transformation of a caterpillar into a butterfly. I told her of my dream and all the roses and feeling Vinney around me in every step. I spoke about all the times I had been graced with meeting family in my dreams, which gave me relief and helped me believe that we never really die. We are only behind the mirror, looking out on our loved ones. That thought can give us strength when times are hard and we are missing someone who has passed away. I brought her comfort. We hugged when she wept, and I felt graced because I could be of help. We lay under ancient beams that night, and I had one of the best sleeps on the Camino.

After a hearty breakfast they waved us off wishing us a 'Buen Camino.' Adjusting my bag, I came across a little old man called James standing in the middle of the road. He had a radiant smile that lit up his deep blue eyes. I smiled at him and he came up and hugged me. I felt my father was right there with us. He was in my dreams and I felt content to have him with me. It is such a beautiful feeling to feel love and not hate for someone whose memory brought nothing but sadness for a long time.

Buddha is right: dreams bring us back to times that we have lived through or are heading into. I certainly had gone back in time, and from these experiences I realise we are souls that are evolving and come back to learn lessons and help society. The biggest lesson I have learned to date is that love is the one thing we all need to survive, regardless of where in the world we come from. We all need love, compassion, hope and courage in our lives to keep moving fearlessly. I also learned that time heals if we let it. Death can be the hardest trauma to get over, but I am a lot more placid around death since I have had so many people contact me, letting me know they are close by (only behind the mirror). I wouldn't be here only for my friend showing me the way in my sleep. I'm sure I will find his message as we move through the Camino. We should learn from deeds that are done to us, both good and bad. Mistakes are what make us who we are. If we learn from mistakes and don't beat ourselves up about a mistake, something that can't be changed, we can move on. I know good people who beat themselves up over things that happened when they weren't in the right frame of mind. Forgiving yourself, showing yourself compassion, that's so important.

Any wrong turn in those mountains could have been fatal without the intervention of people who popped up to help us. The reassurance I got from seeing the butterflies and the memories from other times that helped me make decisions also comforted me. I thought of my father, of how in 2008 he made me listen and acknowledge him. And I'm glad he did, for he also played a part in me ending up on this Camino. Prancing along the undulating road, kicking the dust and enjoying the company of Trish and Claudia, I was feeling excited. A gentle breeze kept us cool and my feet felt a lot better.

You know, when one is healthy and feeling on top of the world, they should be forever grateful. Like St Teresa said, everything changes, nothing stays the same and when it changes it can give us the biggest challenge we could ever face. Some challenges are greater than the highest mountain and it can seem there is no way up and it is too scary to take the first step. But there are many ways to climb a mountain and be challenged in the process. I'll tell you my biggest mountain to date and how I reached the summit with a struggle and jubilation on every step. When we stopped for a sip of water, Claudia asked me what my biggest fear was: loneliness or being on your own. I told her I never feared loneliness because I learned I was never alone, not on the highest mountain or the quietest road. I learned that in 2006 in the Himalayas.

CHAPTER EIGHT

Lhasa to Kathmandu

I spent Lent of 2006 asking for guidance about whether or not I should participate in the Irish-Kiwi mountain-bike exhibition across the Himalayan Mountains from Lhasa to Kathmandu. The priest had put up signs on the noticeboard at the back of the church throughout Lent: the first week, it read 'live life to the full, don't be afraid'; the second week, it said 'have courage'; the third week it read 'be challenged' and on the final week, it said 'just do it'. I had one day left to book the ticket. I rang Vinney and told him I was going. He was delighted and responded with his usual 'onwards and upwards'. That cycle and its spiritual experiences left me in a pure state of grace. I was to learn a lot about myself and my trust in God, and I would be freed of any fears I ever harboured.

Standing on top of Red Mountain, in front of the immense structure of the Potala Palace, once the winter retreat of the Dalai Lama, was breathtaking. It was one of Tibet's major pilgrimage destinations because of the tombs of past Dalai Lamas. Two small chapels, the Phakpa Lhakhang and the Chogyal Drubphuk, dating from the seventh century, are the oldest surviving structures on the hill and also the most sacred. The Potala's most venerated statue, the Arya Lokeshvara, is housed inside the Phapka Lhakhang, and it draws thousands of Tibetan pilgrims each day. Walking within the palace and marvelling at its structure and the beautiful statues gave me goose bumps. The feeling in that palace was no different from any of the giant old cathedrals I had visited, including Santiago de Compostela. As prayers were chanted and carried to the Gods, a humbling feeling ran through me and I was grateful for the chance to see such a magnificent piece of history.

Twelve of us – six male and six female – all wearing green jerseys, helmets, glasses and shorts, stood proudly displaying our bikes, ready for the journey into the unknown. The snow-capped mountains towered over us, and the high altitude meant it was a little difficult to breathe; apprehension engulfed me. I asked St Michael, Our Lady, all the saints and my mother to keep a good watch on us. 'Onwards and upwards,' said Vinney, and we all cheered and started the Camino from Lhasa to Kathmandu.

A highlight on that trip was the monasteries: the Sera Monastery, one of the 'great three' Gelug university monasteries of Tibet, located 1.25 km north of Lhasa and about 5 km north of the Jokhang. The other two are Drepung Monastery and Ganden Monastery. We found ourselves standing among the monks, all dressed in their red cloaks and woollen hats, holding their prayer beads between their fingers. It was an extraordinary moment. We were introduced to one of the elder monks. When he smiled, he radiated pure love and spiritual awareness. A sense of peace and wisdom could be felt from him and around him. When he reached out and took hold of my arm I felt blessed. A very old kettle was boiling on a piece of bent metal. He made us tea and we sat around in a circle and shared experiences. The monks attending school are as young as seven and they run and play and hold hands and learn about scripture. A lot was learned about religion from that brief encounter: its similarities between the holy fathers be they Muslim, Catholic, Hindi, or Protestant or like the Buddhist monks. They all have an innate sense of knowing something we don't and it comes from the same God.

Another highlight and learning curve came on Good Friday. I was struggling to climb a high mountain. My chest hurt from the lack of oxygen and I was having difficulty breathing. I caught up with Vinney, who was also struggling.

'Vinney, do you know what day it is?' I asked.

'What day, Liz?' He could barely speak.

'Good Friday.'

'Halleluiah!' Vinney replied with renewed vigour.

'If God can carry that cross, fall three times, and die on it for us, we will get up this bloody mountain,' I gasped.

We lifted ourselves up out of the saddle and pedalled together, eventually reaching the summit. We stepped off the bikes at 6000 metres and looked in wonder at the mountains surrounding us, towering into the sky. We hugged each other and said 'onwards and upwards to the end'. I shed a tear and felt so graced. For a moment I was transported back to my teenage years, standing mesmerised in the Highlands of Scotland. I had come so far, and I was grateful.

There were a lot of those days to come; thinking of Jesus and the cross made it easier to keep moving and forget the pain, for it was minor compared to His sacrifice. We also had the added motivation that we were doing it for the children with cerebral palsy, in the Holland building in Kathmandu. They needed classrooms for the school, which we would supply with the generosity of people at home sponsoring us. They would be called the Irish-Kiwi classrooms.

A third extraordinary event left me with a free spirit, an open heart and complete trust in God for guidance. The New Zealand group were interested in doing a mountain hike and we were discussing it while the guides were cooking our dinner in two pressure cookers one evening beside our tents. The Kiwis wanted to see the famous Lang Mala, a lookout point somewhere in the depth of the mountains. Despite not having any experience hiking in mountains, my gut feeling was to join the group. We set out the next morning at 4 a.m. with a GPS and flash lamps on our heads. We literally followed each other's footsteps in the snow. One of the group, a seasoned hiker, told me to put my feet into his footsteps and then I would be safe. That was hard to do as he was over six feet tall and had long legs. I nearly broke my neck trying to jump into his footsteps. With the snow up to my knees it was difficult to concentrate on the spectacular scenery. I could hear the eagles hovering above us, looking for an easy feast. I had an urge to stop and admire them. The rising sun lit up the snow, making the scene breathtakingly beautiful. A northerly breeze whipped against my face almost freezing my eyelashes. I wanted to stop, sit and soak up the beauty, so I asked if I could stay where we were and if they could use the GPS to come back and get me on their return. They thought I was crazy, but I felt that God had brought me to this spot for a reason, and I wanted to stay there. A few in the group expressed concern about mountain lions, but I wasn't deterred. I'd share my lunch with one, if I wasn't on the menu myself. There was an igloo-like shelter that I could sit under, and if they could find me again on their way back down, I felt I would be safe.

So there I sat, under the igloo, somewhere halfway across the mountains between Lhasa and Kathmandu. For almost three hours I watched the eagles fly and listened to them sing. I took pictures and meditated on the fact that I was even in the mountains on my own, or was I? I had come a long way in building my confidence with the help of my angels and my friends and my bike. I felt God was preparing me for something and I wasn't to be afraid and trust in the outcome. I even slept after eating my lunch. I felt it was me and God and I was blessed. By then I was full sure we are never alone. All too soon the others came back having reached their view point.

That whole trip, and in particular my 'personal' afternoon in the mountains with God, was very special. I memorised that feeling I had been given and have never shared it until now. The adventure, the people, the helpers and the new friends I made, showed me just what we can do if we really want to, and with trust in God. It was a magnificent experience that I am so grateful for; it has changed my outlook in life. I learned that regardless of the circumstance we should always ask God's help and trust his judgement for the outcome and we are never alone. The Holy Spirit is always within us, urging us to step out of our comfort zone.

We were walking on a stony path, and I considered whether snow would have been easier on the feet. Claudia and Trish thought I had been mad to stay up that mountain on my own, and I tried to explain to them that what I received up there that day lasted forever, and to some extent brought me to that moment with them.

Such experiences do not simply end. We can store them and use them later if we need to.

I tapped into that feeling and meditated on it when I was at my lowest point, during the cancer treatment. It was as if I was on that mountain and remembered the possible mountain lion that never came; he merely watched from a distance. For God was in charge that day and he was showing me his power, for there is none more powerful. That's what got me through the cancer and the treatment and every day since the diagnosis. My spirit was elevated on that journey, and I realised while on the Camino that I was being prepared for the sickness challenge to follow and I'm glad to say I got through it.

'Every day is a good day, regardless of what it brings. See the light and not the dark in everything, hold onto the joy and not the pain. I never spoke about the cancer or the mountain till I started writing. I hope someone will get some courage from reading it.'

'When did you have cancer?' asked Claudia.

'In July 2008. It was challenging, but then all of life is challenging and I'm well recovered and feeling great now and back on the Camino. Thank God.'

'Lord,' said Trish, 'that was some journey, Liz.'

'It certainly was. I don't think I could walk it now, not with my sore feet,' I said, and we all laughed.

'I do believe that the challenges and difficulties we all face, will either make us or break us. For me, my greatest challenge was finding my mother and learning to accept my father's reaction and secrecy around her death.'

'That must have been hard?' said Trish. I nodded my head and kept walking as a tear gathered at the side of my eye.

CHAPTER NINE

Some Journeys Are Not Meant to Be and Some Challenges Are Internal

Although Norway was the planned destination for the summer of 2008 and we were training hard for the mountains, Santiago and St James was never far from my mind. Something was niggling at me, which I felt would be revealed soon. I got the flu and my temperature soared. My symptoms lasted for a month and derailed my training, but I was determined to regain my fitness.

It was an April morning when the letter arrived offering a free mammogram. I decided to wait until I had the time to do it. I believe our relatives hope to help us where it is possible, without interfering with our choice and free will. Even when they have passed away, they are watching us closely. I began to smell smoke and felt someone around me in a strange way, like a shadow. I thought it was my mother, but underneath I knew it was my father; he was persistent in getting me to recognise he had a message. We have the choice to listen or not to our guides. By the middle of May I seemed to be going around in a circle. Something was tapping at my brain trying to tell me something.

One Friday morning I was in the kitchen a bit dazed after awakening from a dream that involved family members, including my mother, father, granny and aunt Lily. It suddenly dawned on me that for some time I kept seeing the words 'health insurance' around me: in adverts, on the TV and the radio. A voice within me told me to check my health insurance. I called my provider and asked what my insurance covered and what hospital I would go to if I was sick. Apparently I would be able to go private in the Mater Public Hospital.

A few days later I received a new policy in the post and I rang to ask why it was so expensive. The same lady told me it was because I had changed my policy. I don't even remember changing it so I was covered for the Mater Private Hospital. The angels and my family were working 'through me' to protect me. I thought little of it and decided to leave the mammogram till later in the year after Norway. But every time I passed the Mater the voice within was persistent: 'What about the appointment?'

I listened and relented. There were at least twelve women of all ages in the waiting room where I sat and read a magazine. I don't like talking to other people in situations like that, it kind of scares me, so I pretended to read and I prayed to St Michael, St Teresa, Our Lady, and my mother and anyone else I could think of. The procedure, though painful, only took a few minutes as they took lots of pictures at different angles. A few days later I got another letter to go back. I remembered the nurse had said that some people got called back for research purposes so I was more annoyed at the inconvenience of having been one of them. I never read the letter in its entirety, just the first bit with the date, time and location. The minute I walked in I realised something was different: it was the presence of men – husbands, partners, fathers. A woman emerged from a room in great distress and I felt sick instantly. A nurse called my name and told me the radiologist would be along soon. I was so confused because I thought I was just there to fill in a research questionnaire. Having elicited that I hadn't read the letter, the nurse kindly explained the procedure. The doctor entered; he was a tall man with greying hair and a sweet smile. A white coat covered his royal blue suit; it was the same colour as St Michael's cloak, which reassured me.

The doctor told me about a shadow and a lump and how they were going to take a biopsy and do some more scans. I felt I was in a movie and the scene would soon be over. I went into a sort of limbo. He asked if someone was waiting for me outside and I told him I had come alone on my bike. He suggested I take a taxi home.

What happened next was like watching a movie on the TV screen, for it was right there in front of me, the picture on the screen. The shadow that was an invasion, that had somehow got into my body, was visible and it was real and not imagined. If someone had asked me where the tumour was, I would have picked that spot. For if I'm honest, for a long time before the diagnosis when I swam I could feel a pull on that side of my body, and when I slept, there was an uncomfortable feeling and I would roll over to the other side to avoid it. I could feel the doctor with his big clampers inside moving around. I lay like a corpse, and I felt like a car having some mechanical work done and I switched my mind to concentration. I asked my mother to take over and think for me. For I felt numb for a while as the noise was making me queasy and the nurse kept asking me if I was alright. When it was over I practically ran out the door, after promising I would leave the bike to be collected. I jumped on my bike and I cycled home.

I never said a word at home. I told my friend and we went on a weekend to Scotland to see Maharaja, the Indian guru that I look to for guidance and inspiration. He was speaking in Glasgow and I didn't want to miss him. There was no point in worrying people unnecessarily until I knew the results. Maharaja's message gave me courage and let me know that all the messages I was receiving were from 'divine guidance'. He never fails me and he speaks from his heart. If you would like to tap into him and see for yourself you will get information on www. wordsofpeace.net. You will be glad you did.

Mary accompanied me to the doctor at the Mater Private. I knew before I went in there would be no trip to Norway, for that year at least. Professor Gorey, a middle-aged, soft type of man with a gentle smile and a sense of serenity about him, arrived dressed in his scrubs, straight from surgery, and he shook my hand and sat down. Mary and I sat opposite him and he told me I had a large tumour, and it was cancer and I would have to have surgery. He went on to say I would have to have treatment, and the amount of surgery would depend on the position of the tumour. I knew his news would not be good, for why else would the spirits and the angels have spent so much time trying to get my attention and telling me to change the policy? Without that intervention I would not have been sitting in his office. In the next breath he offered me surgery that coming Friday. I had little time to think about it.

I looked at Mary and said, 'Norway will still be there when I'm better.'

She nodded in agreement.

Before that week I'd never taken a tablet, except to clear a headache.

Part of the cancer treatment is a tiny tablet that had so many side effects I wondered if it was worth it. I would have to take it for five years, despite surgery and radiation. I was told it could interfere with the melatonin in the brain, the hormone that makes you sleep. I ignored all the other side effects, as they were too scary and best not thought about. Part of recovery is sleep, and mine was so disturbed making it harder to recover and the weakness and numbness that followed for months after was a difficulty.

It was hard to tell the family. I turned it over in my head so many times; how would I say it and who would I tell first? I sat on the sofa staring at the TV and my husband asked if anything was wrong.

'I have to go into hospital as I have cancer,' I replied. Tears started to appear in my eyes.

I'm not one to cry easily. I learned that when I was little. 'What are you crying for?' my father would say in a loud voice, which scared you more. And you couldn't answer because you didn't know how to explain what was wrong. Then if you kept crying he would say, 'I'll give you something to cry for' and you knew it was time to run and hide.

I wanted to run and hide and wake up thinking it was one of my bad dreams. But this was real and there was nowhere to hide.

I don't think it sank in really, as he replied, 'When?'

'Friday morning at six o'clock. The doctor thinks if all goes well I could be out on Sunday.'

'What time on Sunday?' he said, still looking at the TV.

Feeling panicked, I said, 'I don't know yet, he only said might.'

'I'm going to the blessings of the graves in the country,' he replied. 'I can collect you when I get back.'

I almost got sick. He is a man of few words, who doesn't like change, and he was trying to keep normal thinking. His mind hadn't registered what I had said.

'Will you leave me in?' I asked.

'Yes, of course, on my way to work Friday.'

He never asked how bad it was or what doctor I was to see. It's very difficult to know how to react to news that is beyond your comprehension. You go into robot mode. It's one of the hardest things in the world for anyone to comprehend when they are told the news. I guess most people know it could happen to them at any time. Cancer has no concept of time or age. It will show itself anywhere in the body and is getting as common as the computer.

I knew I would have to be strong and trust in God to get through whatever lay before me. I thought of the help I had been receiving when on the bike and the message in the kitchen from the angels. This gave me the courage and the determination to get on with it. There is no hiding place from sickness. As my friend Vinney would have said, 'Onwards and upwards, like a warrior on a mission.'

I downplayed the whole thing with my daughters. Was I kidding myself or denying it was happening? If we dwell on something for too long it will become reality and I wanted it done and dusted so that I could forget it happened. I was trying to spare my girls the worry. There would be no Norway but one always has the choice to go somewhere, and Mary suggested we go to Salamanca after the surgery.

Heading into the theatre for surgery I thought of the lovely feeling I had in the cathedral in Malaga in January, looking at the windows and listening to the music. I felt the angels were giving me something to concentrate on. I acknowledged that this was part of my journey and there were angels on my Camino and I was extremely grateful for them.

Only I could conquer or be conquered with this challenge. I made up my mind I would take every day as it came and I would acknowledge the experiences regardless of whether they were good or not so good and drop them as they passed. I believe if we dwell on bad experiences for too long, we will store them as 'baggage' in our bodies, which will accumulate every day and make us sick.

One of the hardest parts was not being able to swim. I had asked the doctor if I could swim while having the radiation treatment, but it wasn't allowed because I had to avoid chemicals, even those in soap and body creams. As I stood at the bus stop in the rain I thought it was a bit rich of him telling me to avoid chemicals while he was going to pump me full of radiation. Irony and all, I wanted to cry at that bus stop, to let God's tears flow into mine.

I was humbled by the fact that the staff were so caring. They were young energetic nurses and doctors just doing their job, and their genuine caring natures were, in my opinion, over and above the call of duty. I could hear my granny's voice say, 'Earth angels also come in the form of doctors and nurses.' I have been graced by them. And that's a fact.

That whole treatment, regardless of how much love went into dispensing it, washed me out in more ways than one. Towards the end, it was so painful I had to do something to make it bearable, and I used the time in meditation. I gave gratitude for having been given the treatment, and I also prayed for those not so lucky and all the staff that worked diligently in looking after people like me. It is when you are sick that you realise who really cares, and who thinks it is just a burden they don't want to know about. Some people ask in genuine concern how you are, while others ask because they want to wallow in bad news. So I chose wisely those I surrounded myself with, as I wanted to only think in the positive.

In my mind I looked at that cancer episode as if it didn't really exist. I had hidden it under the flag at half-mast: this is what I call the 'storage area' for all the bad news and trauma that happens to people. We hide it; we become afraid to look inside to see what is there, just in case it pops up and we feel the pain once again. My father did that when my mother died. He hid her memory under the flag, stuck it solid and refused to acknowledge her to us children. And when her memory popped its head up, he drowned it once again in alcohol and shut it tight. That was one of the reasons I hated him for so long. I guess for me that episode is one memory I didn't want to be reminded of. I feel he is around and wants to be acknowledged, but I constantly ignore him. Reliving that episode makes me think it was him tapping at my brain and the smoke smell was him too, and so I acknowledged him on the Camino in 2010.

Bad news can have a lasting effect on the brain, and placing these memories on top of the pile can be detrimental to the body. We must have positive thinking and keep charging ahead with lots of plans. It is best to acknowledge every memory and then let it go. St Teresa was right in her wisdom when she said 'Nothing stays the same and everything changes.' Therefore, we shouldn't fret till it is time to fret. Fretting is time wasted and not lived as it should be. We should certainly enjoy the moment and be realistic about the future. We can't hide behind reality by ignoring what is happening; but we can't let it take over either. There must be a happy medium.

St Teresa's prayer, St Michael and another saint called Padre Pio got me through those days and nights. What was the point of being afraid, I thought. Fear will get me nowhere. Face the challenge one step at a time. Like climbing the peaks of the mountain, you have to climb to the top to get the view of what lies before you and look back to see how far you have come. If we took all the challenges that have come our way during our lifetime, add them together and multiply them by the amount of energy we spend thinking about how to deal with them, the total would overwhelm us. These challenges, taken one at a time, can be tolerated with a bit of faith and trust in the universe and a few wise words from the saints or from family that have passed through this life.

That's my thoughts on what has passed and what has to come; I learned that from the Camino. I had always been healthy and strong with no task too difficult, and the pain barrier was always achievable and worth every step when it meant success and goals accomplished.

Our relations are safely at the other side of the mirror telling us it's okay to get worried, as long as we drop the 'baggage' before it accumulates and stunts our growth.

Feel the pain and let it go, stand back and look how far you have come. I know that my mother was also involved in getting me to notice the events leading up to the diagnosis. I have asked for her help many times throughout my life and I pray to her all the time. We all have the ability to have contact with the angels and our family who have passed before us. We must be open minded and always be on the lookout for the signs that are all around us if we so wish to heed them. That is our choice. I am so glad they kept at me and I listened. I'm sure if I hadn't I wouldn't be here to write this.

I now give thanks to all the people that helped me throughout that time. In particular Mary my buddy, my two daughters, Lesley, Celine, my husband and the extended family and all my friends without whom it would have been more difficult. I had the surgery and although it was distressing and painful I'm thankful for it.

CHAPTER TEN

Salamanca and Fatima

Mary and I were sitting in her kitchen having coffee and contemplating what we would do now that Norway was on the long finger. We were looking at the map and decided our journey was to be to Salamanca in Spain for prayer and thanksgiving. A visit to St Teresa's convent that she opened on 1 November 1570 was on the cards too, as well as a trip to Fatima to Our Lady.

Mary and I arrived at Salamanca with great excitement. We stood in the huge square and marvelled at the beauty around us. A reflective blue sky that mirrored onto the ground made us think we were upside down, and the golden background was stunning. The city has one of the oldest universities in Spain, dating back to 1100. Mary studied there as part of her theology degree and was excited to go back and meet friends. We headed to the apartment, kindly provided by one of Mary's friends. From the window we could look out over the rooftops and watch the sky change colour.

We decided to take a bus to Alba De Tormes where Santa Teresa was buried in the church next to the convent she opened in January 1571. There was a museum dedicated to her and St John of the Cross. We sat on the bus admiring the landscape. The dry brown sandy roads stretched out throwing dust into the sky; greenery was scarce and scattered giving the landscape a sense of the desert. The church steeple was visible from a great distance – an icon directing people to Santa Teresa's convent.

We knocked on the door of the museum with excitement and apprehension. It was opened by a little nun of about four and a half feet tall. She was very old, possibly ninety, and she had a smile that lit up her whole face and a grace about her that is hard to explain. She was humble and she seemed to radiate light from her eyes as she moved along the corridor with us in tow. She reminded me of the Tibetan monk I had the privilege to meet while in the Himalayas. There is something in their eyes and their body language that is hard to explain; a knowing about them, like they know something about life we don't, something mysterious, and it's about God and love.

She walked silently and quietly, and it was plain when she spoke that she was dedicated to Santa Teresa. I felt like Santa Teresa was working through her, still doing God's work. I thought it funny how the people in her time should take out Santa Teresa's heart, cut off her index finger to put in caskets for people to see in the future; the sight made me shudder. There was a mass of personal things belonging to her and I felt like I was intruding on her privacy. We saw her books and pens and her walking stick. I expected her to walk in the door at any minute and ask us what we were doing, and I kept looking around. There were paintings on the walls of people of the time in the sixteenth century and a spectacular big statue of Jesus on the cross. We moved throughout the memorabilia, mesmerised and humbled, tiptoeing in the silence as if afraid we might disturb someone. A look of surprise crossed Mary's face and my heart missed several beats. Out of nowhere, a very beautiful butterfly landed beside us on the table. We were gobsmacked as it was dark and we were indoors. Clearly it was a message, as Santa Teresa talked extensively about the butterfly and the struggle it had to develop from a caterpillar into a butterfly. I felt she was saying 'keep going and all would be well'. We looked at each other in amazement.

We proceeded to the church of St John of the Cross situated in the square. St John of the Cross was a Spanish mystic and a Roman Catholic saint, a Carmelite friar and a priest who learned the importance of self-sacrificing love from his parents. His father gave up wealth, status and comfort when he married a weaver's daughter and was disowned by his noble family.

It was out of poverty and suffering that John learned to search for beauty and happiness not in the world, but in God.

I felt privileged and inspired as we went inside and prayed for health and a safe journey through whatever was ahead of me. I knew I was being told it would be tolerable and I was reassured that all the saints knew the struggle for they had all had struggles in their lifetimes. St Teresa had lost her mother and turned to God as did St John when his father died. I felt they knew our struggles for they are not much different to theirs. Mary lost her father and I lost my mother as young children therefore we had a lot in common with each other and with the saints. Such was our contemplation we nearly got locked in the museum. Thankfully we didn't, and more importantly, we didn't miss lunch.

After a hearty lunch of fish, salad and dessert, we went to the castle and I climbed up the tower and looked out onto the countryside. I thanked God for the day and asked Santa Teresa to continue to watch out for us and help St Michael, as he had a hell of a job looking out for us too. When you are surrounded by these nuns and feel their grace and see the love they have for God in their eyes, it is humbling.

Fatima was the place to rekindle my soul, ask for guidance and contemplate the rest of the year ahead. Not being able to go off on the bike and still being apprehensive about the outcome of my treatment, I was glad to go there. This was to be our 'pilgrimage', to thank Our Lady for my recovery from the surgery and for all the times she helped us in our lives, both on and off the bikes. I felt very humbled and excited at the prospect of taking the train there. I remembered the time in Lourdes when I was helping out, pushing the wheelchairs and having fun while praying for everyone that asked me to pray. This time it was my own intentions and the intentions of all the people who prayed for me when I got sick.

The train was held together with rust. Saddened old carriages squawked like caged birds as it slowly moved. I tried to rest, but it was an impossible task with my insides rattling in harmony with the repetitive bumping. One man was snoring, oblivious to the smell of perspiration, cigarettes, food and cheap perfume. We stumbled down the carriage in search of coffee. Holding the rail above our heads, I felt like Miss Marple on the Orient Express. There were people of all ages perched up against the walls and children were asleep on bags stretched out across the floor. Mary and I were laughing, not that it was funny, but at each other for some reason.

The train halted and everyone piled out and climbed into a waiting bus. The bags were thrown into the boot. The hour-long bus journey was more comfortable than the train. Everyone was on a mission: to get a seat in the church. It was strange that although there were so many children, not one was crying. Afterwards, we walked in line with people from all over the world. They spoke so many languages, a smile and a nod was enough for communication. Everyone moved swiftly around the large racks holding hundreds of candles. When the holders are full the candles are thrown into the fire giving rise to the flame of hope: a flame to burn the sorrow. Prayers are said and heard in many languages as people, deep in contemplation, move around in slow motion.

There was commonality in gratitude and prayers, and there is no language barrier when one is in the presence of Our Lady. The joy felt can be recognised and acknowledged without words. Hope is written on people's faces and visible in their eyes. I believe that no matter where we are at any moment regardless of how we feel, calling for God's help is the key to keeping our sanity; that and remembering St Teresa's words: 'Everything changes and only God suffices; He helps us charge forward with hope in our hearts and peace in our minds.'

Being in Fatima filled us with hope, for I believe that without hope there is nothing. When we realise we are at a hurdle and need all the help we can get, prayer and faith can get us over any challenge. Fatima was my place to be thankful when I was half way over the biggest hurdle I had yet to face. After the surgery there was the waiting game, for the treatment and the final outcome. I felt I was in mid-air, and I could either hang there in fright with 'what if's' or have fun and enjoy the journey every step of the way. I chose that latter, for every minute in life is priceless and irreplaceable. I wanted to enjoy it.

The next morning we walked along the river bank in the lovely sunshine, filled with hope. There was a flock of birds in the giant trees singing their song and a mixture of beautiful coloured butterflies dancing their dance. We sat down to have a coffee and were smoked out of it; too many people smoke in Spain and we were so used to smoke-free zones it was hard to take. It reminded me of my father who smoked one after the other and the smell would make me feel sick. I would say, 'Daddy, they will kill you' and they did. I felt him around me on that trip. I felt he was trying to get my attention.

The memories of the trip to Fatima helped me when I was having the radiation treatment. I visualised Our Lady and all the people praying. It was like a chorus of angels in my head. Having something positive was important especially when the pain was hard to tolerate. The pain of radiation is necessary pain to help prolong your life. But the pain we all carry in the form of 'baggage' every day in our hearts is not necessary. I believe that's the pain that makes us ill and that is where the roots of sickness started in me. When my mother died, we children were kept in the dark by the family regarding her whereabouts, and we learned to worry and live in fear we would be sent away. So much unnecessary pain and anguish was harboured over ignorance and dominance of religion and family values that were old-fashioned and based on shame.

I still find it difficult to talk about that which happened fifty-nine years ago. It's one of the memories that is at the bottom of the 'baggage' file and is hard to dig up. I hope this Camino will give me the peace I need to talk about it without the aching memory. I never looked at the cancer episode in the light of 'why did it happen to me?' We all have a journey, and we're all going to get some type of sickness; few are lucky enough to get by unscathed in this life.

I think how we deal with our burdens is what matters. When I was at the hospital I noticed there were young women having treatment and some of them were as young as thirty. At times older women sat waiting for their daughters who were having treatment. This sight would open your eyes to the extent of the cancer that is attacking women and men all over the world. I would say to people that if in doubt get it checked out. Don't take no for an answer when they tell you, you are too young for a mammogram. I know of one person who had three mammograms before the cancer was detected. It was detected only when her mother persevered in her dreams telling her to go back and she did, and she was diagnosed and had her treatment. That was more than twenty years ago and she is still going strong. Mammogram machines are much better now thanks to research.

That episode and its journey has left me stronger in mind with my faith elevated and my understanding of this world we live in is clearer in my mind. I'm not saying it was easy to come to this conclusion. This is the first time I have looked at this episode in detail and the only time I acknowledge it now is when I see the doctor for a check-up. I leave the hospital grateful for another year and slip the memory under the flag that is now easier to lift up and acknowledge the trauma. It's easier to settle during a trauma that although happening and painful we know will come to an end. We all need comfort in God's help and the help of St Teresa, St Michael, Buddha, Allah or the sun and the moon – whatever gives you comfort. The words of St Teresa to let nothing disturb you and nothing frighten you, and all things will pass, were particularly powerful for me.

I guess Margaret Solis was right when she said the Camino can drive your mind into turmoil and unleash everything that is hidden in the depth of our soul. Remember there are lots of hidden treasure in their too. Brian Keenan, in his book *Four Quarters of Light*, said, 'There is one truth I absolutely believe, it is that the mind forgets nothing!' The subconscious mind is always active and we need to learn to stop it in its tracks when it brings up the negative. For me, with my experiences I don't believe anything happens by chance! I believe that we are led and guided for our journey. If we fail to connect to the next part of the journey and listen to the spirit for guidance and move fearlessly, we will miss out on so much of life that can never be repeated. To fail to move forward out of fear will cause our hidden dreams to smother and dwindle like the ashes in the fire. You can never go back on the Camino, but you can look back and learn from your experiences and make a decision at a crossroads to change your outlook in life and move on fearlessly.

The heart that is closed is like a lifeless fire, and it is a sad heart. A sad heart hosts a soul that is alive but asleep like a dormant volcano. But if as adults we can dust back the ashes, the sleeping desire will gently awaken, showing itself once again, and will burn with desire for life and love.

CHAPTER ELEVEN

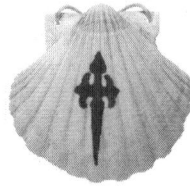

Padre Pio

Padre Pio was canonised in 2002, the year I went to Vietnam and requested his help in the midst of a fearful moment. I was first introduced to St Padre Pio by a little girl lying in a hospital bed in Dublin. She was six years old and was dying of cancer. I was visiting her with a friend and a priest came into the ward.

'How are you today?' he asked the child, who was clearly unwell and not long for this world.

As he blessed her with holy oil, she replied, 'I'm okay, Father; it's you that needs to mind yourself. Padre Pio is looking after me.' She pulled a picture with a piece of his glove attached to it out from under her pillow.

I was amazed at this little girl's faith at that stage in her life. Padre Pio must have been comforting her. That was my introduction to St Padre Pio and later on a friend gave me a medal with a piece of his glove on it. For years I wore it around my neck every time I raced my bike or ran a marathon, and I still take it with me. It's funny how things are synchronised in our life if we make the connections with different times and places and people we meet.

In 2002, I was cycling in Vietnam with friends, including Vinney and Mary. We had cycled for more than two weeks in sunshine and without a mishap. A storm was forecast and the weather changed dramatically. The TV showed a massive storm approaching Hanoi, where we were headed. A plan was put in place by the government to protect whatever could be protected, as there was fear of the country being flooded. We still had two more days on the bike before reaching Hanoi and the final destination. For the first time in that journey we became concerned, and Mary was awake during the night, worried about what we would do if we got caught in the storm. We assessed the situation the following morning and agreed to use a van if it became too dangerous to cycle.

We had arrived at China Beach, a beautiful place along the coast, where fishermen invited us out onto the sea with them to fish. I swam in the China Sea that evening among the high waves. The rainbow-coloured coral was beautiful, and the children sold it at the side of the road. However, when I got out of the water, my Padre Pio medal was gone. It was lost in the sea. I couldn't believe it; I had swum in lots of sea races with it around my neck and worn it to many countries without losing it. I felt there was a reason for this, and I said to Mary that maybe it was a warning; maybe we needed to pray to Padre Pio, Our Lady and St Michael to keep us safe, which I did that night in bed.

I decided not to swim the next morning; instead I packed my bags in preparation for the journey. One of the men travelling with us, a very good athlete and a friend of Vinney, came in after his early morning swim. He looked fresh and was full of mischief. He offered me something from his closed hand. I jumped back away from him, fearing it was a spider. He laughed, opened his hand and there it was – my Padre Pio medal. I couldn't believe it and I realised then that there was nothing to worry about. It was a sure sign that all would be well. The storm ended up changing direction and we finished our trip without another drop of rain.

I believe that was a miracle and ever since Padre Pio takes pride of place in my house.

The stony road was quiet and Trish, Claudia and I were flagging. It was time to keep our eyes peeled for an albergue. With a big smile on her face, Trish told Claudia that she and I had visited Padre Pio's village in Italy that previous year. I had wanted to spend my sixtieth birthday there, close to him. Claudia looked surprised; I suppose it's not everyone's idea of a birthday destination.

'What a trip we had,' said Trish. 'We were graced there, weren't we, Liz?'

'Without a doubt,' I replied.

If you've ever wondered if you were truly being watched by the angels then we had the proof. We were taking pictures and laughing, having fun on the veranda of the lovely house we were staying in. The countryside was beautiful under the red and blue sky. The sun was beaming its rays on top of us. It looked like every time we moved the sun's rays moved with us. When we looked back at the pictures we were amazed. There was an 'orb' beside both of us in two different pictures and one that looked like it was being carried in a beam of light floating in the sky. I believe this type of thing is a sign of angelic presence.

Claudia wasn't at all sure what I was talking about, so I was happy to show her a photo I had taken a few days previously while we were walking through a forest. There was one in that picture too. She also seemed surprised that two Irish ladies would have such an affinity to an Italian saint.

'The Irish love him,' said Trish, enthusiastically.

'That's true,' I said. 'We both gave Padre Pio pictures to people when we came home last year, and they were delighted and wanted more,' I added.

'That's a fact,' said Trish. 'If we'd had a suitcase full of them, there still wouldn't have been enough to go around, such is the love people have in Ireland for him.'

He is a saint of our century and had the greatest challenge of all – to bear the pain of Christ in the form of stigmata – and he bore that pain for fifty years without complaint. When he was alive and people were near him they got the smell of roses. Perhaps Vinney was trying to say to me to remember Padre Pio on this trip, with all the roses about. I guess he is with him now enjoying his company with his beloved wife. I felt tears form in my eyes as I imagined his smiling face in front of me.

'I'm blessed to be here,' I said to Claudia and Trish. 'I think all those trips I made were in preparation for this one.'

'Didn't you cycle the route?' Claudia asked.

'I did, but that was different,' I replied. 'It was important, but it was different.'

CHAPTER TWELVE

In the Right Direction for a While

In July 2009 Mary and I embarked on a cycle, beginning in Brittany. I was nervous because I had taken a tumble on the bike at home some time before, and I was still recovering from treatment. It was Mary who spurred me on, and as I sat in silence with her in the basilica in Brest, in front of a statue of St Teresa of Avila, I felt true gratitude. My fear dissolved as I remembered the beautiful quote that I think was found beside her bed when she was dying: 'Let nothing disturb you. Let nothing frighten you. All things are passing away. God never changes. Patience obtains all things. Whoever has God lacks nothing. God alone suffices.'

We were facing into torrential rain and I was nervous. A beautiful butterfly passed by and I felt a shiver run down my spine. We were being watched and guided. The butterfly closely mirrors the process of spiritual transformation: we all have the possibility to be reborn through retreating from the world into our inner being, surrounding ourselves in a cocoon of prayer and meditation, which will in turn assist us and give us the reassurance needed when faced with the unknown. Butterflies don't live very long, a few weeks or months at best, which reminds us that life is short and moves quickly.

Our few days in Brest did not go well. Instinctively I felt we were being led on a particular journey, because we had not successfully reached any place we had set out to find. We booked a train ticket to Bordeaux and planned to cycle to the station the next morning to get the 05.50 train. We decided on 'night flitting': to get on the road early to avoid heavy traffic. The train journey was action-packed: our bikes kept falling around us as there was nowhere to store them; we were falling around while trying to steady the bikes; the conductor pushed us back onto the train in order to make us descend from the other side, and someone stole Mary's camera from one of the panniers. That was upsetting, as she had many photos of her family in it. After a quick visit to the cathedral where I saw a statue of St Catherine (a saint I needed to learn about), we found some accommodation and gladly put the day behind us.

The following morning the streets were buzzing with walkers and cyclists intent on the Camino di Santiago. The signs of yellow arrows and shells were everywhere. We wished those we met a 'Buen Camino' and enjoyed the excitement. Our exit out of the city was fraught as the signs were totally confusing and we had to retrace our steps and start again. After cycling for most of day without really knowing where we were going, we were both relieved to see a large statue of St James in the middle of a crossroads. Pilgrims were arriving from all sides, backpacks swinging on their tired bodies. When I complained about the perspiration seeping down my back, Mary replied, 'It's a pleasant change from the rain and the cold.'

'We are going from one extreme to the other,' I said and laughed as I approached the statue, which brought a smile to our faces. He was leaning towards the direction of Santiago de Compostela. One would think he had been in a hurry and was stopped in his tracks. The mere sight of him gave us a lift, and we got excited and I felt he was indeed leading the way, egging us on to get on the road to Santiago.

We walked into a lovely twelfth-century building where a lovely man with dark wavy hair stamped our Camino passports. He directed us to the next stop, which was twenty-six kilometres away. Cyclists can complete more mileage than the walkers before stopping off for the night. We cycled through a national park, a huge tranquil forest with a wonderful path. Pedalling seemed effortless. There were rows of tall trees standing to attention like soldiers, and the smell of flowers and trees was intoxicating. Mary and I began to sing, 'Oh Mary we crown thee with blossoms today, Queen of the Angels and Queen of the May.' The trees danced and waved as we sang those words; they were acknowledging Mary, Queen of Heaven. Oh, how we loved her. I have loved her since I was seven years old. She is my mother and your mother, everyone's mother, the Queen of Heaven and earth. The birds seemed to join in too with their chorus. It was like a choir of angels.

Time flew and we arrived at a small bed and breakfast. There we met a quiet French lady called Marion who was walking with her two-year-old Labrador. She was quiet at first until Mary and I began to talk of our adventure, and not knowing where we would end up. We shared some food and she confided that her journey was to help her deal with a failed relationship.

'I'm walking to find peace in my soul,' she said, with a look of sadness in her eyes.

I told her life is a journey and not a destination and she should reach inside and find all the good things that happened in her relationship, and learn from the bad ones, let them go and move on.

Another young girl from Canada arrived; Maria-Ann was a student and had read about the Camino while on holidays. This was her second day. She wanted to challenge herself, and, being young and inexperienced, had walked almost thirty kilometres. She practically collapsed into our arms and was extremely tired and hungry. We sat her down, shared food with her, helped her unload her bag and get into bed. She was tucked up and asleep in minutes.

'That's our good deed for the day, Mary. Let's see how many more we get en route,' I said.

We slept on bunk beds in a very small room. It was very cosy, all of us sleeping together with a dog there on the floor. I had a great night's sleep and awoke refreshed at 6.30 a.m. The birdsong outside enticed me to get up and open the window. The smell of pine was hypnotic. There was something nice about sleeping in that small enclosed place, surrounded by the forest. It made me feel safe and secure. It was like reliving the adventure in the Highlands of Scotland when we stayed the night in the bothies, and cooked ourselves food, waiting for the ranger to find us. I tried to get dressed, but the room was so cramped it was difficult. The dog was licking Mary's face. I laughed out loud and pulled him off. She wasn't used to dogs, certainly not waking up with them washing her face. I went outside to play with him as the others dressed;

he was full of beans and full of love. Sitting outside, we had breakfast of fruit, bread and coffee. It was lovely looking at the shadows of the trees in the twinkling sunlight. We said goodbye to Marie-Ann and Marion and the dog and wished them a 'Buen Camino'.

The National Park Forest looked divine as we headed into its centre. The trees went on as far as you could see, and the aroma was breathtaking. The animals were all out, birds were singing, rabbits were running and the pilgrims were moving as if hypnotised by nature. Butterflies were everywhere, hordes of them, reminding me of the abundance of angels that are at our calling.

Two and a half hours of sheer bliss ended with a motorway and hordes of traffic. The peace was lost and for about twelve kilometres we were praying again, asking for God's holy help as cars and lorries flew by like aircraft. Total concentration was needed, and when we pulled up into a side road we were frazzled, hot and shaking. I guess there are always two sides to everything! Ups and downs make the world go around. With that in mind we walked to rest the mind and body. The perspiration ran down our backs and I had to keep reminding myself of the rain and cold that sent us there.

With eighty kilometres complete, we stopped at a little village; it looked like a holding of farmyards all clustered together. The sun shone on a tall building with sandy slates that was painted red and green. Walking around the building we spied a sign built into the wall: the shell representing St James and the Camino. Smiling and nodding to each other, all thought of the heat and the sweat disappeared and we took a picture and knocked on the door. The lady came out, looked at us and beckoned us in. She led us to a room at the top of the house; it was like a barn, with a pyramid-shaped window looking out to the sky.

After a shower and a change of clothes, our hostess, Maria, served us a delicious dinner of fresh soup and salad and vegetables, all picked from her garden. We were the first ladies to arrive that year and she was delighted to hear we were Irish, as she didn't have many Irish staying with her as a rule. After dinner we went for a walk around the streets; it was a beautiful place, quiet with lots of houses and well-kept gardens. There were no people out though. The trees and the whole ambiance of the place had so much spirit it was like you were waiting for something to happen and were not sure what. I felt there was a sleeping giant waiting to roar. The smell of fresh grass and the birds singing practically overwhelmed me with gratitude. I thanked God and the angels, in particular St Michael, for guiding us there. I had been calling on him all day; just to remind him we were on the loose. The more I see of the world the more I am enticed and believe that God truly is in everything, and in everybody. Maria is one of the workers of St James who takes people into her home, feeds them, gives them a bed for the night and sends them on to the next place.

We woke at 7 a.m. the following morning to a storm. The pyramid window was open and the whole place lit up with lightning. The rain fell in sheets, like a waterfall. It was beautiful to look at. I was excited as falling water never fails to give my heart pleasure. We lay back on the bed enjoying the sight in safety, jumping when the fork lightning lit up the sky making a noise like crackling geese in flight. There was no way I was going out in that and neither was Mary. We sat for an hour in sheer bliss. The rain slowed up at about 8 a.m. when a rainbow circled the sky.

The smell of coffee coaxed us downstairs, and we enjoyed some fresh fruit, bread and jam. By nine o'clock the rain had stopped totally and the ground was drying fast. There was not another person in sight, and we settled the bags on the bikes and moved off slowly, warming up the legs in preparation for a journey into the unknown. Everything looked fresh and the birds were out singing in the trees. We stopped at a small village to buy supplies for lunch. We decided to have a coffee while looking at the map to decide our next stage. Two French pilgrims entered and spoke to us. The men asked us where we were heading, and we told them we were undecided between two routes that ended up in the same place: Saint Jean Pied de Port in the Pyrenees. One of the walkers, David, seemed to know a lot about each of the routes and he advised us to stay on the original route; it was hillier but had less traffic and was safer. They were our first angels in waiting and only for the storm we could have missed them. I decided to look every day for people like them or symbols such as butterflies and any other yellow arrows and see how many guides were looking out for us. I would call on St Michael to intervene if we got stuck or were unsure of the next step to take. The sun was rising and the heat rose, promising a beautiful day ahead. Prayers of gratitude and a song for Mary Our Lady was on the agenda. We both agreed we were blessed coming to that part of France, considering we picked it out of desperation. I thanked God for the rain which drove us there.

The rest of the afternoon was gruelling and was spent in silence. By 1.30 p.m. we stumbled upon a place called Dax. The narrow street was eerily silent; everywhere was closed and there wasn't even a place to shelter from the sun. We sat on a doorstep to eat our sandwiches. When a police car appeared and pulled up beside us I took the opportunity to ask him about a bike store. Mary's bike had snapped a brake cable and needed some brake pads. It was too dangerous to go any further without them, and we were heading into unfamiliar mountains. Once you are heading into mountains you need everything in order and your wits about you.

By the time the shop opened and the bike got fixed it was 4.45 p.m. I felt we should stay in the town and start again fresh in the morning. Mary had other ideas; she wanted to climb. I was feeling very tired and I had pins and needles in my arms from holding the handle bars. I had taken another bike, not my usual one, and it wasn't as comfortable as the old one. It put a lot of strain on my shoulders, and I couldn't figure out why, as it had been measured for size. I relented as Mary was insistent that we keep going. Once she gets a notion about climbing that's it, but I was wary and had a feeling from looking at the map that the mountains were high.

After five minutes on the road, realisation set in, and I knew it was the wrong decision. The road wound upwards and around and I prayed to Michael Archangel to keep us safe and lead the way to a safe destination. Up we went, a hell of a climb that must have been more than two miles upwards to the first ledge and to an opportunity to catch our breath. Climbs are tricky at the best of times, but with tired legs it was nearly impossible. Having two and a half hours off the bike, and then trying to make the legs feel good and work especially after fifty kilometres in the morning, is against nature.

We dismounted and walked. The road seemed to be dragging us. I felt I was going backwards even though it looked manageable. At the top, there was a junction with roads going right and left and a blank forest wall ahead of us. Mary had a call of nature and she threw the bike in the grass. Instantly there was a hiss. The front wheel had hit some thorns and the tyre deflated in slow motion. Mary is a true cyclist, with many mountains and continents in her legs, but when fixing a bike, she takes her time. So I left her to it and watched the butterflies around me. I also knew a decision would have to be made regarding which road to take, and I was desperately looking for a sign. I called on my mother and St Teresa and all the saints whose churches we had visited.

With the bike repaired, Mary asked, 'Well, right or left?'

'Right,' I replied. 'That's the road the cars are taking.'

By that stage we were hungry and our legs were sore. We climbed for another two miles when the same tyre deflated. There were a few houses to the left of us, but what caught my eye was a very large camper van in a garden. There have been many times during other trips that St Michael sent his help in the form of an earth angel with a van. With that thought, I knocked on the door of that house. There was no answer and we walked away, but something told me to return and try again. This time a woman in her forties emerged. We gestured towards the flat tyre and to the camper van. Another woman came out and I got the feeling they were a couple. They were so kind and piled the bikes on the back of the camper, directed us to sit inside and took us to the nearest accommodation, which was quite far away. We would never have made it there ourselves so late that evening. I also noticed on the way, that there wasn't even a place where we could have pulled over and slept in a tent for the night. We truly would have been in dire straits, and without a bit to eat.

We arrived at a 300-year-old bed and breakfast in the middle of the mountains that was owned by a lovely Belgian woman called Annie. I asked Annie to tell the lady she was our angel and she smiled and nodded her understanding before she took off back home. We wanted to pay her and she refused the money. We insisted, and she took €20 for the diesel. Her kindness saved the day and St Michael was with her all the way. He must have a very special way of communicating with van drivers! I thanked him silently and asked him to keep up the good work of minding us. The kindness of people who go out of their way is not always acknowledged. There is always the bad news, which focuses on the negative, but good people are everywhere.

The bed and breakfast had such character. Every inch of it seemed to have been built with love. There was a gentleness to it, and I knew we'd be well looked after. The décor inside was antique and so tasteful. Annie led us to the bedroom where there was the biggest bed I had ever seen. The gardens were visible from the bed. We lay down exhausted. Almost in unison we said, 'All we need now is a swim.'

My grandmother's gentle voice came to me. She always said that

'If we are grateful to God for the small things in life, he will know we appreciate them and he will give us all we need, when we need it.' I felt her beside me and I hoped she enjoyed the journey.

Showered and refreshed, we went downstairs, where we were met by Annie and her black curly-haired dog. I missed my own dogs so was delighted to give him a cuddle. Annie didn't provide dinner for guests, so we rang an Italian restaurant nearby to tell them she would be dropping us down there. After a lovely meal of fish, salad and a giant pizza, Annie came back to collect us, which was so kind of her.

Her husband, Mike, was there when we arrived back. He was a wine connoisseur by trade and opened a bottle of red for us to enjoy together in the garden. I could hear the insects singing and they were buzzing around our heads. Mike was telling us some history of the area and how they came to have the house. It was very easy to chat to him. It felt like chatting to an old friend and catching up with each other's adventures. He was very knowledgeable about history, and he listened in amusement as we recounted some of our tales and adventures.

'Tomorrow you can have a swim in our pool and we will get the bike fixed for you. You look as if you need a rest,' he said, as he proceeded to turn on the lights which lit up the whole garden. The garden was beautiful, high trees and plenty of grass that was cut to precision; every stem looked the same height and there were lots of sheds. We looked around in amazement and saw a lovely swimming pool, surrounded by a tiled patio. I couldn't believe it. Annie reappeared and asked if we had taken a rest day since we had started. When I said we hadn't, she suggested we stay with them for another day and accompany them to their friend's house the following evening for a barbecue. I couldn't get over it: one minute we were in a crisis on top of a mountain, the next minute we were in a chateau sipping wine and looking forward to a swim in a pool. The Camino is full of God's helpers, all intent on helping others reach Santiago. Needless to say, we accepted the invitation.

By eight o'clock the following morning we were at the swimming pool. We just lay in silence and looked up to the blue sky and I thought I saw a falling star, or was it an angel? Mary was reading her book and I was engrossed in Shirley MacLaine's book about the Camino. Annie had breakfast ready; the smell of fresh coffee and fresh bread and the boiled eggs were most welcoming. Annie said she was heading to get the bike fixed. She had printed a map leading to Santiago for us to look at.

We decided to explore a medieval castle nearby, which felt oddly familiar to me, and we walked back through the fields of maize that looked like clouds of gold ready for harvest. Dinner was a joyous occasion and we were made feel so welcome by their friends. We felt like family. I guess we are all family when it comes to it, God's family, regardless of what country we come from.

God bless Annie for she had washed our clothes and they were waiting for us the following morning. I felt sad almost, as we said goodbye. We had been so well looked after and I felt we had not repaid them as we should.

Back on the road, we spent twenty minutes climbing when we should have been going downhill. Eventually we retraced our route and settled into a lovely cycle. After three hours my gears slipped, and Mary nearly came off the bike beside a car. She had been cycling alongside me, chatting and singing. After that incident I kept back as I had a strange feeling it would happen again. I kept a good eye on the bike, my ears were open and my mind was focused on the moment. The route was very good at that time; there wasn't much traffic but a fair few large hills to climb and descents where the scenery would take your breath away. I felt very good in myself, stronger after the rest day. The hills were getting bigger and turning into the mountains of the French Pyrenees. We kept going and were extremely happy.

Eventually we came upon a lovely statue of St James in the middle of a street. We got excited and I could feel my heart beating at seeing him. It was so reassuring to see him. His very presence gives you courage and determination to forget the pain. We were about twenty kilometres from Saint Jean Pied de Port. I knew I was being led somewhere and I was just enjoying the climbing even though by then tiredness had set in. Just before the top of a climb I heard a voice inside me telling me to change my gears. I thought it was really strange because you don't change gears until you are ready to descend, and I was still climbing. I got to the top and changed gears immediately, and at that moment the chain snapped and wrapped itself around the wheel. I nearly went over the handlebars. I shouted at Mary to stop as I landed on the ground with the bike on top of me. She stopped and came back to me. We looked around us only to realise that there was a ten-kilometre drop in front of us. I nearly threw up my coffee at the thought of what might have been. Had I not heeded that voice, I would have been mincemeat. Without a doubt, my mum, dad and all the angels had intervened. I was truly grateful.

We stood in silence, both wondering how we would get out of this one. For some reason I had packed a set of tools called the 'buddy' that my friend Terry had bought me for Christmas. Oh, I missed him then, for he was the one who normally did these things for me. Thankfully, I had watched him fix a chain five years previously while cycling in Scotland. We were perched in a very small area and it was difficult to manoeuvre. We both prayed to Our Lady of Lourdes.

Eventually, I did the best I could until I could get to a bike shop. We freewheeled down the mountain, only to be met by another. I was sure I heard a whisper in my ear and the goose pimples stood on the back of my neck. We got off the bikes and began to walk up the next mountain. I felt there was someone beside us and I could hear noise like the pounding feet around me.

Those roads are ancient and they are known as the Roman Roads. The Romans walked these roads for centuries as did many other people from around the world, all on the way to Santiago de Compostela. Their ghosts were now guiding the way; perhaps I too would have walked that road and guided future pilgrims had I tumbled down the mountain. I shuddered at the thought. We freewheeled down that mountain and walked up yet another. It was difficult and I felt like a donkey carrying the weight. The road had beaten us and we were walking as one should on the Camino according to tradition.

Descending at forty miles an hour was one of the scariest things to do. I had done many of these before but not with a chain that I knew could give way at any second. It is like everything in life: if we are not aware of the dangers we are not afraid. As children we move about fearlessly in the world around us and treat it as an adventure park, until something or someone tells us otherwise.

I could feel a slight disappointment as I knew I would not get to Santiago on that trip. Immediately an inner voice assured me that perhaps God knew better, perhaps this was enough for me at that time, perhaps I needed to realise that my illness and treatment had taken its toll. I was pushing myself to my limit and He knew it. The last descent was fast and furious. It led us directly into the town of Saint Jean Pied de Port, right to the door of a bicycle shop that was closed. Right there and then I knew I was being told to finish in the mountains.

The fact that it was St James's feast day was not lost on me. That evening we sat in the church, watching peacefully as pilgrims lit candles and offered up their intentions. Singers and musicians played to celebrate their saint. It was sheer bliss. I thought Mary might be disappointed because we hadn't travelled our usual 'hundreds of miles' and she wanted to cycle over the mountains to St James. But I felt him there – all around us.

When we returned to our farm accommodation that evening, I must have prayed for an hour in gratitude for all the help we had that day. I couldn't sleep at first. I watched the stars in the sky and the lovely bright moon out the window and eventually drifted off. Thankfully I had a peaceful sleep, and I realised I was learning to take things as they come and not worry about the outcome. It had taken me years to attain this type of peace. I felt it had come in the mountains, in particular the Himalayas. I had taken that peace to the Pyrenees and, hopefully, when I returned to Spain, I would carry it with me all the way to Santiago.

CHAPTER THIRTEEN

Pain of the Personal

Our feet were sore, making our bodies sore. I suggested to Trish and Claudia that we needed to find somewhere in the shade to rest. Within half an hour we came upon a café and hostel that had a wall of roses climbing the side of the building and tables outside in the shade – a perfect place to rest. It was very quiet. Trish suggested we stay there for the night, which I agreed to, but Claudia said she had a hotel booked further along. We would be saying our goodbyes after she had rested. We removed our footwear to let our feet breathe.

'St Teresa said that pain is never permanent,' I murmured to myself. 'And see? Already my feet are less painful.'

'She's very important to you,' Claudia said.

'She is,' I replied. 'She also said "To have courage for whatever comes in life – Everything lies in that." St Teresa said these words while her own health was diminishing, but she continued her travels throughout Spain to open up her convents. In her writings in the "Interior Castle" she said, "Humility is the ointment for our wounds because if we indeed have humility, even though there may be a time of delay, the surgeon, who is our Lord, will come to heal us." Aren't those beautiful words and if we look at them together they make sense. I found that when I was on the bike or walking in the mountains and when I had the surgery for the cancer. I prayed for courage and assistance, and I have been entirely grateful for every bit that came my way, including you my friends for having patience and walking slowly and listening to the story and not rushing the Camino.'

Just then, thanks to a gust of wind, the smell of roses engulfed us and I felt my friend Vinney around me, accompanied by St Padre Pio. I felt so blessed in that moment.

'St Teresa missed her mother's love and she replaced it with God's,' I said.

'Why do you refer to the loss of her mother so frequently, Liz?' Trish asked.

'I believe my love and curiosity of God came the day my father told me I should go to Mass. My need to love in my life came through the absence of love at home; it was never expressed. The loss of my mother shut my father's heart and he blamed God for her absence.'

'Why do you think that?' asked Trish.

I paused, wondering how I could explain this further to Trish and Claudia. It was personal, but by this stage I was feeling blessed and peaceful, willing to share further. I explained that while I was freewheeling down the Pyrenees with a dodgy chain, I was regretting all the gear I was carrying, that on the next journey I would need to detach myself from some of my favourite clothes and things that I always took with me. They were weighing me down. I wondered why detachment was a struggle for me, and as my Camino with Mary finished in the mountains I realised this struggle was linked to the death of my mother.

'If this is too hard, Liz, please don't push yourself to revisit painful memories,' Claudia said, but I shook my head and continued anyway.

My mother (Kathleen Bridget Brown, née Connolly) died in childbirth in 1958 when I was twenty months old. My sisters were eight and seven, and my brother was three and a half. By the time I was four, both my sisters had also disappeared from my life. Her death left an innate torment in the family, and it started in my father, George Brown, then aged thirty-one. Growing up, I overheard vivid details that I was too young to understand the significance of. One phrase, in particular, never left me: 'She lay with her baby locked in her arms, asleep forever.' My siblings would say over and over, 'Mother went away, she died and she never came back.' I concluded that to die was to 'go away' and I lived with this feeling that it was somehow 'our fault' she went away. Our mother's death would have a profound effect on each member of the family. Some members even after almost sixty years rarely uttered a word about their feelings or how they coped with her absence. Not being told where she was or had been brought to for her resting place caused mayhem in our young minds. My two eldest sisters decided to not go to school for fear our mother would come home and find them missing. They would enter one gate and exit another, running home to check if she had returned. This behaviour went on for almost two years. During that time my grandmother stepped in to help look after us, along with other members of the family on a short-term basis. We even went into a 'residential home' for children. I don't recollect the time in that place; but my sister can verbalise every detail. The memories are imprinted in her mind, such was the trauma from the experience.

My father had a second chance of love and a stable family if he had opened his heart and thanked God as opposed to blaming him. He became engulfed in loss until it was too late for him to realise his mistake. That I believe is what he is trying to tell me with his messages from the grave. That love came through my mother's sister Elizabeth (Aunty Lilly) when she came to stay with us. Despite their having a beautiful baby boy together, my father couldn't see the chance he had been given with her. Lilly was my godmother and looked like our mother. She had long black hair and her warm smile was reassuring and comforting. She was a shy placid person who lacked confidence to talk back to my father. He dominated her and used her like a servant and yet she ran the house with her own money, which she earned by working in a factory doing heavy manual work. I called her 'Mammy' and I was happy as one would expect a young child to be under the circumstances. That happiness lasted till I was four years old. By then I could understand more of what the other siblings were saying. They talked about Mother going away with the baby and not coming back.

One day someone got angry with me calling her 'Mammy', saying she was 'Aunty Lilly'. I don't believe I called her 'Mammy' again after that. Everything changed from then on. I began to look at my mother's picture and wonder where she went. I would clean it when no one was looking and beg her to come back. My mother was snatched away before I could even remember her smile or the feel of her hand in mine. From then on it was only in my dreams that I could remember her vividly. Her spirit was always in our house and in my dreams. I could hear and feel her. When I was very young she would talk and I would listen. She kept me quiet and in a state of innate happiness.

My father, having taken the tragedy so bad, had his own troubles to deal with. Something had died inside him that left him hollow. His hollowness would shape the rest of our lives in one way or another. Everything, right down to our very basic human needs, became a 'chore' and led to a heated argument and an excuse to go out and drink. He drank and smoked to kill his pain and mask the hollowness. I believe we were constant reminders of our mother, and that was hard for him. He never spoke about her other than to look at the empty chair and ask why God took her away. At these times I would ask him where he took her and could we ask for her back. He would growl and send me out to make him tea and so I stopped asking. For years I wanted to ask him why he could not share just a little of his memories of her with us. His silence caused me to hate him more as I grew older. One day my father, without knowing it, gave me the greatest gift that would get me through my life: he told me that my mother wanted us children to be Catholic. He was Protestant himself, but he said she had faith and I was to go to Mass and learn about God. He began to send us to Mass and even gave us a penny for the plate for the priest. It was the first time he had referred to my mother while sober, so I listened.

I realised very young that God was very important, and that He and the angels were by my side to give me courage, courage my father never possessed as he became lost forever in grief. His grief meant there was no healing for anyone because her memory had to be hidden and never spoken about. My father never considered the grief and pain of his children. Sometimes his grief would lift momentarily. During those occasions I would sit on his lap, talk nonstop and ask him so many questions that he called me a gramophone. I never asked the question I so badly wanted to ask for fear he would storm out of the house and be sad once again, and it would be my entire fault.

When I was four, I heard loud shouting and then my mother's voice telling me to run into my bedroom and scream. My father was inside beating my sisters for not going to school. I screamed and he stopped. I saw tears and confusion in his eyes. That night was the last time I was to see my two sisters for five and six years. One was nine and one ten years old. There was no talk of them during those long years, so I drew my own conclusion: they were dead and had gone to my mother and I wanted to join them. I realised during one of the Caminos that living with a ghostly silence caused us to be terrorised of someone disappearing through death. I had wanted to die too so I could go and find them and persuade them to come back.

The house changed then with my sisters gone. My father became more demanding and drank even more. The house became lonely and scary, but I could always hear her voice and feel her presence around me.

It was many years before I learned where my sisters had been taken. I was married when my sister told me the story of their confinement and the treatment they had to endure. This story made me grateful I was too – young to be sent away and that my aunt Lilly looked out for me. They had been sentenced by a judge to spend five and six years in an industrial school in Aberdeen for missing school. The reason being 'they never went to school.'

The judge said they were 'looking for their mother' and that was why they never stayed in school. He sentenced them to five and six years in this industrial school. My father's mother asked for them to be sent to the nuns in Nazareth House. The treatment, the beatings, my sisters endured there was far from what my grandmother had envisaged. They weren't allowed to come home for holidays because the nuns disapproved of how my father was living with my aunt without being married. These nuns abused and bullied young, innocent, vulnerable children who had been put in their trust. My aunt Lilly gave up her life to look after us. She was the greatest 'earth angel' to have ever walked this planet. She was full of love, but my father couldn't detach himself from the memory of my mother – to honour it as opposed to covet it.

I believe we must become able to detach from each other and from experiences. This is important if we are to live as we should 'in the moment', enjoying every precious day. Closing his heart prevented him from loving and enjoying each new day. I believe he was afraid to love for fear it would be taken away from him. Burying feelings caused the accumulation of baggage that built up over time and suffocated him, making him ill. All my siblings and I have accumulated such baggage throughout our lives. Fear is the largest piece of baggage that can attach itself to a person; it can paralyse them, render them immobile to life itself.

I know that throughout my various Caminos my father was present and he was looking for forgiveness. It took me quite some time to even allow him to be 'heard or felt' within my heart, never mind to consider forgiving him. I couldn't detach myself from the hurt he had caused me.

*

Understandably there was silence when I finished speaking about my family. I was surprised I had said all I had, and the others were lost for words. We watched the people stopping to admire the roses that were hanging on the wall of the café. I thought of Vinney and the lovely way he had said goodbye to his wife despite being in the midst of grief, and how he had urged the congregation to love their wives and families. He felt the love of God and never blamed him.

'All this thinking has stilled my brain. I've a headache. I think I'm dehydrated,' I said, reaching for my bottle.

After a lovely few hours together, it was time to go to our accommodation. We took some photos, promised to stay in touch and said our goodbyes there in the shade. Claudia is an 'earth angel'; she loves all the people she looks after and sees them as family. As she left, she reminded me to keep writing.

Every day we wake up to the unknown, even when we think we know what's happening. The Camino is no different.

Orbs are angelic lights, a sign that you are being looked after.

Humble dwellings are found all along the Camino. Open your heart and you will never be without a place to stay or food to eat, no matter how low your budget.

With my good friend Mary Ryan, one of my besties and my Camino companion.

With my sister Kathy, collecting our certificates after the our Camino from Portugal to Santiago. I hope I have inspired her to do more.

The higher the mountain we climb, the deeper we find ourselves.

Every day is a good day, regardless of what it brings. See the light and not the dark in everything; hold on to the joy and not the pain.

CHAPTER FOURTEEN

The Northern Camino –

Finally

inally this was it, the journey to Santiago and St James. I hoped that this time there could be no mishaps with the amount of angels lined up to help and guide our way. Mary and I left Ireland on St James's feast day – 25 July 2010. I would have loved to spend it in Santiago but we always seemed to be either starting or finishing the trip on the 25 July but never in Santiago.

We were to begin in Biarritz in France and take the northern route – Camino del Norte – along the coast to Santiago de Compostela. I was told that this was a good route used by many cyclists because the roads were smooth and the sea would make it cooler on the hot days. Time would tell! The thought of a cycle and a dip in the ocean every day for weeks was enticing; along with the mystery of the angels leading us to safety at the end of each tiring day.

It wasn't long before they were called upon. After our bikes and bags had gone through security, Mary discovered the long-handled wrench in her back pocket, which we needed to attach the pedals to the bike on the other side. We couldn't let security take it away. Panic set in, and the prayers began. Within a few minutes there was a bit of commotion up front. Down the stairs came the man in charge, a middle-aged athletic type. After an explanation he informed us he was a cyclist and had done the Camino, and yes, he let us through and told us not to tell a soul. He was our first earth angel.

Almost immediately in Biarritz I realised I had too much baggage. We cycled to Saint-Jean-de-Luz (St John of the Light) to our accommodation, Hotel Paris. Then we went to the church of St John the Baptist to get stomps in our Pilgrim's Passport. As it was St James's feast day we wanted to catch Mass and light candles for everyone on our list. It was a magical start to our Camino. That night I dreamed of my grandmother and of saying to her that I hoped she was proud of me. She told me to enjoy the journey. Mary woke me up at 5.45 a.m. and we went for a swim in the sea an hour later. The coastal road through the Pyrenees presented us with many climbs ahead. We had to deal with busy motorways and difficult climbs out of the many towns we met along the way. There were some very scary parts, as there was nothing between us and the sea apart from plunging clifftop drops. Looking down into the sea from a very high height made me dizzy, and it was difficult to admire the scenery because to take your eye off the road could have been fatal.

We stopped for lunch at 1 p.m. and our brains were frazzled from concentration. Our legs were in good shape, though. We continued on towards San Sebastian but had difficulty with some confusing signposting. On one occasion there were two signs for the one place pointing in two different directions. The twinkling sea in San Sebastian was tempting, but the yellow shell sign of the Camino and its arrow spurred us onwards, and we didn't pay heed to the time of day. Suddenly we were climbing high up and the bike was struggling because my legs were tired.

'Mary, will we walk a bit of the way?' I called out, remembering the punctures we got the last time we headed into the mountains.

We stepped off the bikes and walked. The mountain was so steep and seemed to go on forever, up and up and up. I was beginning to wonder if there was an end to the mountain or if there were any houses in the area.

'The arrow did point in this direction, didn't it, Mary?'

'Yes it did, straight ahead,' she replied.

Two cyclists came down on the opposite side of the road. They stopped and looked at us and said, 'Too much baggage to carry'.

We laughed and agreed with them. They told us about an albergue for pilgrims twelve kilometres ahead, at the top of the climb, and wished us a 'Buen Camino'. Courage, stamina and determination were warranted, as there was no sign of a van!

When we arrived at the gate at seven o'clock, we were met by earth angels in the form of a lovely lady and her family. They came out to the gate, took one look at us and beckoned us inside. Her back garden was full of people eating around tables. They waved to us and said 'Buen Camino' in French, German and Spanish. We were the only English-speaking people there. It was such a lovely welcome. However, when the lady of the house informed us that she was full, we panicked; where would we sleep? The lady had a conversation with two dark-eyed teenage girls who were serving the dinners, and it was agreed that they would sleep on camp beds and give their room to us. Needless to say we were eternally grateful.

This lady was very special. She had a bright smile and her eyes were full of love. My heart filled with emotion as I felt her look after us. She reminded me of my grandmother. After a hearty meal, I sat content on the swing in the garden, surrounded by trees and looking out over the mountains. A black and navy sky was lit up by the moon. Most of the other pilgrims were washing clothes in buckets of water, while catching up with the day's adventures in various languages. Mary was among them practising her Spanish. I thanked God for looking out for us once again. I contemplated the amount of things I had with me and how few we had used the day. The cyclists were right; I had too much baggage. What could I do now but only carry it?

As I watched the other pilgrims, I remembered how much my grandmother loved hanging clothes on the line.

'Hang them upside down and watch them blow in the wind,' she would say. I could see her in my mind's eye, standing back admiring her effort, arms folded, enjoying the sun on her face. My granny was making her presence known to me, and had done so right from the start of this Camino.

Growing up, I viewed my granny as an icon. Her family moved to Scotland during the famine and like her father, she worked in the mines during the First World War. He didn't think it was a job for a woman, but she was no ordinary woman; she was tough and strong, unafraid of hard work. She met my grandfather and married him without her parents' approval. She was a rebel in her day, a strong woman with her own thoughts, and by the time we the grandchildren came along she had wisdom and knew how to pass it on.

She helped me in many ways, in particular when I was seven years old and anxious to learn to read. At that time in the early 1960s, the teachers spent more time putting the kids outside the classroom than trying to teach them. I was feeling deflated after a battle with a teacher who told me I was stupid, illiterate and would amount to nothing. At that time I could hear a voice inside me I assumed was my mother's that said, 'You aren't and you will.' So I told my teacher, 'I'm not and I will.' This enraged her and I ended up calling her a witch. When I told my granny the tale as we peeled vegetables for soup, I saw her smile as she turned her face away. I knew she was laughing. Then she told me firmly that I would learn to read when I was ready and I would never stop learning.

'If I live till I'm a hundred, I will still be learning, for if you are not learning you must be dead,' she said, with a big smile on her face. 'Everyone learns at their own pace, and nobody knows everything, only God.'

I adored her. She lived until she was eighty-four and, along with my father, was one of the best teachers I ever encountered. She was invaluable after my mother died, and we would be so excited to see her coming off the bus laden with goodies when she visited. She always bought me a doll in the summer. I had bride dolls, baby dolls and Croly dolls, which I guarded with my life. I loved her hats and the hatpins that I felt went right through her brain. I often stood mesmerised, watching her put them in place, adjusting them, as she stood looking in the mirror, and she never even batted an eyelid. To me that hatpin was almost the length of her walking stick and twice as sharp. My grandfather died from TB in the middle of the Second World War, leaving her with six children, one of whom also died of TB. Those traumatic events must have been heart-wrenching for her and I remember hearing her say, 'The lamp is inside and we must learn to keep it lit, regardless of what the day brings. Trust in God and all will be well, and keep the lamp lit, even in times of sorrow and heartache.' My grandmother had the ability to detach the pain of baggage, remain faithful to Our Lady and God and lead a fruitful life. I missed her very much when I came to Dublin at eighteen, and I looked forward to her letters. She knew I loved to go to the church, and she said to pray to Our Lady. She knew that praying helped focus the mind, especially when one is lost in pain. I was so glad she was making her presence known on the Camino. How could we ever feel lost knowing we have so many people looking at us from behind the mirror?

The next morning, Mary and I dressed in silence and packed up the donkey: that's what I was calling my bike by then. I realised that the house was called St Martin; he'd made his presence known to us the last time in Biarritz. I pointed that out to Mary, telling her he was another saint with us looking for recognition. We were reluctant to leave that albergue as the energy was so positive and loving there. Mary and I, along with Vinney, had experienced a similar feeling in Vietnam. We'd come upon a large extended family in a small tent near China Beach. They had very little but welcomed us with love and the offer of some tea. When love is around in abundance, there is a feeling of contentment and lightness in the heart, which was my thought for the day.

The road started out with some cobblestones and a large hedge above us on both sides. We were both feeling apprehensive and it was visible in our movements and lack of motivation to move. I'd never felt that way before; it was a sick feeling almost. It was like one was leaving a safe place and going into the unknown. We wondered if it was an omen, so we said our prayers and chose the track road off the main road because that was the one with the Camino shell signs. It felt safer, and almost immediately we both felt better. I acknowledged the fact that we were being guided. Suddenly, just as I was settling into the cycle, we started downhill. It was scary because we were on a thin ledge high above the ocean and had to trust wholeheartedly in the angels to keep us upright. We arrived in Getaria in the Basque region, a picturesque place with a beach winding around the bay in the shape of a mermaid's tail. While we had lunch we laughed about the amount of prayers we had said getting there. After we paid the bill, a young man appeared and told us the best route to take as he had done it before.

'Another guide, Mary. The angels are working hard keeping up with us,' I said.

I was fully convinced he was our angel. I had seen lots of butterflies all around the track road and remembered the mountain in the Pyrenees with the butterflies and the puncture, and I knew all was well and we had nothing to fear. They were all waiting at various destinations.

'What wonder,' I said to myself as I moved off pedalling the bike. We were heading along the coast for Debá, a town of important architectural heritage that boasted a jewel of Basque Gothic architecture: the church of Santa María de Debá. As we climbed to the top, low and behold, Mary got a puncture right beside a statue of Our Lady of Mount Carmel. I felt we were being told to acknowledge Our Lady and St Teresa. After the puncture was fixed we reached Debá. An eerie feeling ran through me causing me to shudder; there was a strange sense of being watched. Standing at the tourist office waiting to stamp the card, we eyed each other in a mirror and began to laugh and hug each other. This was an emotional journey with another part of the Camino completed safely.

A young man gave us directions to the albergue for pilgrims but we got lost. Thankfully an older gentleman put us right and brought us to the albergue which was up two elevators. We had to squeeze in one at a time. These elevators were not made for bikes. After exiting the elevator we had to climb up a path of cobblestones, up and up and up we went, sliding about on our shoes. It was so difficult with the bags. The nice man carried them up for us, after he freed Mary from being caught between two cars. I was pushing my bike and trying to pull hers as she pushed from the other side; she was in fits laughing. I was trying to control mine, as I was afraid I'd let the bikes fall on top of Mary. Tears were running down our faces as we sat at the top, having said goodbye to the nice man. He wished us a 'Buen Camino' and headed down the elevator. Then Mary announced she had lost the map, which was the second one. That made me think once again that we were definitely being led, and I thought if we never acquired another map we would still get to Santiago de Compostela. Life is full of ups and downs, and just when we think all is good, another hurdle awaits us. That's the trial and tribulation of living in this world. At that moment I realised we must embrace every moment, good or bad, happy or sad and make the most out of them, for they are all learning curves, leading us on to the next part of life's journey.

As we were first to arrive at the albergue we had the pick of rooms; there were eight beds to each room. The view below served as a reminder of how high we had climbed. After placing our sleeping bags on our beds, we went back down to the town centre. Mary had to buy some glue because the heel of her sandal was loose. People watched us in amusement as we were sitting on the footpath waiting for it to dry. Standing in the sea after a much-needed swim we laughed over the happenings of the day. When we returned to our accommodation later on, I became concerned about the lack of curtains on the window. I was worried about being able to sleep. Then a young French lad of about twenty handed me his eye patches. I was so grateful to him. People are always criticising our young people about their behaviour and lack of respect to older people. I admit there is an element, but that is very small and the majority of our young people throughout the world are angels in disguise given half a chance.

The room was peaceful, as all the walkers were tired out. There was a sense of security about the place, like a family of all age groups, from different countries, sharing the humblest of lodgings and all with the same purpose in mind: to get to Santiago de Compostela, regardless of how long it took or how difficult it would be. We would all need God's help and the help of all the angels that surrounded us. I was not going to be shy in calling them for guidance, and I would acknowledge their help at all times.

By the time our bags were packed we were the last out the following morning. There was great difficulty getting the bikes down the slopes, worse than getting them up, as we had been helped the previous night. We kept sliding about in the shoes. Eventually I took mine off and took the bags down one at a time, going back for the bikes. Mary was minding them and setting up the bike when they arrived. Then it was the elevator; we were laughing so much at this stage trying to fit them both and ourselves in with a squeeze. At the bottom, I realised my glasses were on the ground at the top of the first elevator. Mary went back up again, leaving me laughing and fixing the bags to the bikes. At last we went to a café for breakfast, but by this time it was ten o'clock and I was already tired and we hadn't even done a mile. I felt a bit sick with the breakfast – too much moving around I thought, not enough relaxing time upsetting my stomach. After buying a tyre tube at the bike shop we were finally on our way towards a small village, whose bells rang as we passed by. Heeding the call, we stopped at the church and went inside where we were given the opportunity to read a UCB Christian booklet. It contained some lovely passages. We decided to wait for lunch and just watch the children playing and the parents chatting. Their slow pace of life reminded me of when I was a kid and we would play all day without a worry in the world.

The scenery in the mountains was beautiful and I could hear the birds sing and could smell the flowers. I could almost hear the mountains call out to me to slow down and enjoy them; instead we were in a hurry again, motoring along as if the devil was after us. We encountered a church of ancient beauty that had the names San Miguel (St Michael) and Eliza. Built with stone and wood before the Roman Empire, it held traces of damaged walls and paintings with missing faces and shaded backgrounds from the time and smouldering fumes left from the war.

A shiver ran through me as the face of St Michael smiled down at me – a reminder of who was in charge of this trip. Having God in one's life is like having a shining star glowing inside us. God is in everyone, and when we are happy, so too is God. I felt humbled and entirely grateful to St Michael for giving me the sign I needed, and I acknowledged the fact that he has always kept the bad demons away. I was being told that all was well. I remembered a very nice man in Egypt who told me my name was Eliza in Egyptian. I had the most amazing feelings in Egypt and I met a young girl of twenty, with the darkest of eyes that seemed to look right through me. She was extremely spiritual for her age, and she said to me that we had met in another lifetime. The hair stood on the back of my neck because the night before I had dreamed of living there.

Symbols are all around us, we just have to take notice and piece them together. Deepak Chopra, in *Synchro Destiny*, reminds us of Aladdin and his lamp. If we are like children and believe that lamp is within us and we acknowledge it, our deepest desires will be met and our soul's destiny achieved. Deepak reminds us that everything that happens in the universe starts with intention. I felt God intended us getting to Santiago and I would acknowledge him on the journey. With this in mind I sat back in contentment and ate the fruit and drank the water from the tap in the square. It was so hot I could hardly move. And the lamp inside me was saying, 'What's the hurry?'

The kilometres were moving slowly and I felt I was using more energy than was needed. Eighty kilometres felt like two hundred with the extra 'baggage' on board and the stress of the traffic. I thought back to the message in the booklet, which said, 'As we set out today on the journey we should trust in God; just as Jesus trusted in God his father, that all would be well.' With that thought I was very happy then to keep going and keep praying.

People are the only 'animals' that long for more, of practically everything, be it material or physical, as in a challenge: like us anxious to get to the next stop. We wanted the adventure and I think for me there was a deep-seated need to succeed and challenge myself to the limit. I guess I wanted to prove the cancer had not done any harm or changed me in any way. A challenge is only a challenge when it is done with courage and faith. Santiago had become an obsession with me. It was that focus that got me through, as my patience was running thin with the mountain of traffic. Pulling into a little village, I noticed it was being suffocated by the building of apartments. There was no place for pilgrims. We hovered around, not quite sure what to do next. The traffic was so bad, I would have slept in the tent on the footpath rather than get back on the bike. As we stood on the side of the road looking about in dismay, a nice man with an apron on advised us to keep going, as it was only eleven kilometres to Bilbao. I had lost count of the kilometres with the stress of the traffic and exhaustion setting in. I remembered the word for today being 'trust in God' and I immediately realised I had let fear in, and it had taken over for part of the journey. Fear has a habit of popping up when we let it; fear can be the devil knocking at our brains, especially when fatigue leaves us vulnerable.

I thought about my time in the Himalayas, when it was God and I and the eagles, waiting for the mountain lion that never turned up. I trusted in Him wholeheartedly. It was there I realised that the longing I felt as a young child for the mountains was in my blood. I must have known that someday I would be rewarded for my constant longing and imagination that inspired me as I sat on the church rooftop, looking at the mountains that surrounded Glasgow. I acknowledged the main thing for me, which is that I love God and I know he loves and looks out for me. With this in mind I thanked the man and we set out again with a bit more confidence.

The first thing we saw was the steeple of the basilica of Santa Maria. The bells were ringing for the start of the Mass and we entered. The priest prayed for pilgrims on route to Santiago. There were at least forty in the church from different countries; some had flags hanging from their backpacks. When it ended, a middle-aged man with a mop of curly hair directed us to the centre of town. The man warned us about the large steps and suggested the alternative route down to the plaza. Of course we missed that, and, yes, we ended up going down the steps, bump, bump, bump all the way. We weren't laughing as we were tired and not able to think clearly. A nice young couple in their twenties came down and took the bikes; they looked light when they pushed them, that's because we were tired. Silly really, I thought, as I looked over to my left and saw the other road hidden behind trees.

CHAPTER FIFTEEN

The Northern Camino –
Challenges and Churches

'In all our necessities, trials, and difficulties, there is no better or safer aid existing for us than prayer and hope.'

— St John of the Cross

Bilbao is an industrial port-city in northern Spain. It is surrounded by green mountains, which were hard to admire because of the traffic on the way into the city. It's the de facto capital of the Basque Country and is famed for the curvy, titanium-clad Guggenheim Museum which ignited the city's revitalisation when it opened in 1997. We arrived at the oldest hotel in the city, Le Petit Palace, where the young man, upon realising we were pilgrims, rushed to take our bikes and put them safely away. Michael was his name, and he couldn't do enough to help us. After we freshened up, he gave us a map of places to visit and we left in search of food. We were overjoyed at having landed once again on our feet, truly led and helped along the way. We looked forward to the prospect of a day off the bikes to explore Bilbao.

The next day I awoke at 8 a.m. after being tormented by dreams. Mary slept well as she does and was ready for anything; it's hard to keep up with her when she is in flying form and full of wonder. We headed out with sore legs, laughed as we could hardly move them forward, such was the build-up of lactic acid in our muscles. I forgot the map, but I felt it was better to be led out to the day and see what it brought.

The beauty of Bilbao is breathtaking. Santiago cathedral was standing tall over the city. The temple is consecrated in honour of the apostle Saint James the Great (Santiago in Spanish), by virtue of being a point of transit for the pilgrims that followed the northern branch of the Way of Saint James. That beautiful building holds so much history, and I surmised that this was only a small part of what awaits pilgrims in Santiago. The Camino was certainly showing us surprises. We turned the corner of the main road by the water front and there in our midst were three churches – St John of the Cross, St Michael and St James – all three saints letting us know they were looking out for all who travel the Camino.

'That's freaky, Mary,' I said. 'All three of them were in my dreams last night; they must want to be acknowledged.' I opened a very large old book with a leather cover. It reminded me of a book I opened when I was a child in a bookstore while changing books for my father. We read about a museum of the immaculate conception of the church, and off we went to investigate. There was a large double room full of artefacts dated from as far back as the twelfth century. There were riches of all kinds in the form of windows and furnishings. The workmanship that went into building them was splendid. St Michael was there in splendour. There was one large statue of him dressed as a woman, and did I get a shock at that! Mary took a picture of him and me and we laughed because we looked alike.

Was it coincidental that we should come across that statue or was it part of the planned journey, to reassure us on the way that St Michael comes in many forms? Was that why I could hear his voice? A middle-aged priest came to speak to us. He was a bit lonesome as he was new to the parish and missed his old one in Salamanca. We said we would pray for him and asked him to keep us in his thoughts. He wished us a 'Buen Camino' as we waved him goodbye and walked out of the church. We were standing on the street admiring the outside of the cathedral when a couple of nuns came up beside us and we began to chat. They were called Carmel and Elizabeth and they were heading to Santiago with a youth group to raise money for Aids patients. They were very happy young nuns, very caring in nature, and they both showed great love for the people they worked with. These nuns were doing God's work and were so happy to do so, even though they would be sleeping in the streets sometimes. The Camino has many people crossing it from one direction or another. Some people are oblivious to their own pains or suffering, as their hearts are full of empathy for others, and they recognise and trust God for support. These people work through love for each person and are free of fear because the angels are guiding them. Meeting people like the nuns on the Camino was good for us. It gave us a sense of reassurance of not being alone, that at every corner there were people helping each other. Tired out and filled with joy from our day's findings, we headed back to the hotel.

Before we left the next day, we lit some candles in the church of St James. I had a sense of innate joy at what lay ahead. Putting on our helmets and glasses we wished each other a 'Buen Camino' and laughed as we stepped over the bike and toppled over.

'We couldn't very well go wrong on a straight road down the river, could we?' I said to Mary, as I took off feeling apprehensive.

I felt a despondency enter my heart at leaving the Bilbao; there was a sense of mystery and security in it and I promised to someday go back and enjoy its treasures and not be in a hurry to leave. Suddenly, we found ourselves in the docklands, surrounded by large containers and parked lorries. We barely had time to take our feet out of the pedals when out of nowhere came a nice young man who told us we were headed for a dead end. We had missed the turning point on the road. He looked like St John of the Cross: soft eyes, round forehead and his hair receding at the top of his head, coming around his ears like a halo. He led us safely out of the place without question. We followed his car for about five kilometres. He waved goodbye and wished us well – our first angel of the day and another soul to remember in our prayers. Once again the road followed the river, and we could see the mountains surrounding us in the distance. A lovely gentle breeze brushed my face and I felt safe. I felt I was kissed by an angel and I thought it was my mother; she had been on my mind that night.

Our next helper was Maria: a lovely lady in her forties with a big smile and dark hair. She had good English because she had worked in England for a couple of years. She too pointed us in the right direction. By midday we stopped and entered the church of La Virgen María de las Mercedes. The artwork inside centred on the angels; they were all around the church and they were beautiful. All the archangels were dressed in bright colours. This find left us elated and we lit the candles and prayed for everyone on the list, including St John. I always feel that to pray for someone's intention and actually feel the person's need from one's heart will get the attention of the angels, in particular Archangel Gabriel, as he is the angel of communication and he will carry the request to God. On reflection, I realised that all the saints en route that appeared in any form needed our prayers, and they were there not only to help us, but for us to help them. I decided that each time I came across their presence I would acknowledge them, not only for their help, but for their intentions.

The end of the river brought us to the car ferry, the local transport that takes people to work. We stood squashed in between a variety of age groups from infants to old people who kept looking back at us. I guess they had never seen two 'ladies' like us with the bikes and the baggage. Walking off the ferry, a nice young man pointed in the direction for the next part of the journey. I couldn't believe it; escalators, big long escalators, slanting to the right of me like a mountain on an incline. People just stepped onto them and they brought them up over the incline.

'Another hurdle for us, Mary,' I said, as I tried to get the bike onto it, but it was too narrow. We looked at each other and began to walk alongside them up the grass path. These escalators were there to bring people up to the village as it was built on a mountain. Everything seemed built on a mountain in Spain.

We were definitely the topic of conversation at the dinner tables in many houses that night. People looked in amazement as they sped by us on the escalator. We pushed the bikes with great difficult up alongside them. The sweat was pumping and my legs were clearly not happy with the load being forced on them; every nerve was shouting in objection. The church steeple stood out among the houses; it was a welcome sight. We headed there for a rest and shelter to find Santa Clara inviting us in. St Clare became the next saint leading the way, helping to break the journey. She was the first Franciscan nun to follow St Francis in the twelfth century. More prayers were said and more workmanship was admired. I was glad of the rest. As we left our next helper appeared. The middle-aged man pointed us in the direction of a beautiful cycle path all the way through the mountain.

After another hour of cycling, a great feeling of excitement shot through me when we arrived at a lovely beach. We placed the bikes against the wall and sat down. We drank some much-needed fresh orange juice and ate some olives to hydrate and replenish the electrolytes in the body. Searching for a sign for the pilgrims' accommodation, a nice young lady pointed us in the direction across the sand. Thanking her, we looked in dismay and realised we had to push the bikes across the sand – another hurdle. It was so difficult because the sand was soft and it piled up around the wheels. A large population of families relaxing on the beach having picnics were looking at us, and I could see them sniggering. I didn't blame them; we looked comical.

On arrival we were given a warm welcome at the accommodation. It was run by volunteers and a donation of €5 was the cost. This village was called Pobena. Two volunteer girls came out to meet us and they pushed the bikes to the lock-up. Being welcomed by strangers who are lovely people always makes me feel humble. I sat back on the nice comfortable bunkbed, and prayed in gratitude for the help. The shower was glorious. I stood in the steam, drenched in gratitude for everything. Water, I love it, in any form! Ready for some fun, we headed up the street to investigate the town. It was a bank holiday and there was a traditional festival on where people dressed in clothes from centuries ago. We bumped into people from Germany we had met in Orio at the albergue; there were nine of them, all family and friends. The youngest was eleven and she was doing great, walking without any bother. One of the female members had hurt her ankle and it was strapped up. She was afraid she might not make it to Santiago and was contemplating what she would do next. A young girl took a picture for us for her memory bank and I stood and watched the lovely yellow butterflies dance around behind her. I felt the angels were saying, 'Well done, you made it once again.'

The accommodation had so many beds in the one room they were on top of each other. It's like a silent movie at times in the sleeping quarters. People are so tired they go about in silence, organising things for the next day's walk. It was a difficult task for us to go about in silence; we liked to talk to people and we always found something to laugh at. As we all lay down it was so silent you could have heard a pin drop. I felt the presence of the angels and the saints keeping people still and resting. For a second night I felt I was being told to slow down, savour the moment and enjoy the journey. I promised myself I would try to make sure to meditate on the journey every day. Life can be so hectic that it passes us by and we are not even aware of it. It can be a little complaint about something so trivial like it is raining, or it is cold, or it is hot, and we fail to see the big picture that life is wonderful regardless of the weather. Just to be alive is a gift and nothing short of a miracle. We should constantly acknowledge and be grateful for this gift.

By 7 a.m. people were shuffling about, getting dressed and preparing for the day ahead.

The place was packed out and they had to put extra mattresses on the floor to cater for the crowd. I was sitting on the top bunk bed, trying to dress in the confined space and pack up the bag at the same time. Mary had dressed and was out of the room in the toilet. There had been a German man sleeping on the bottom bunk bed below me and we thought he had left. During the night he had gone to the toilet and Mary woke when he was walking back inside. She thought it was an apparition and she proceeded to crawl over into my bunk bed shouting and frightening the wits out of me. At that moment I had actually just fallen asleep. He looked very strong when he lifted his bag up onto his back to leave. The same man came back in to talk to another German man and check he hadn't left anything behind him. He bent down onto the bed and picked up something. I couldn't make it out at first. Just then, Mary came strolling back into the room and she proceeded to squeeze in behind him to get to the bed, as she had dressed beside his bed thinking he was gone.

In broken English and a smirk on his face he called out, 'Who owns this?'

Mary reached over from behind him and timidly said, 'I do.'

She reached up and retrieved her bikini bottoms. I almost fell out of the bed with laughter and the man went off about the day with a grin on his face. We laughed so much we were last to leave the dormitory. The hostess was telling everyone to leave by 8 a.m. and we were dragging the bags out the door and laughing at the same time. We hadn't even time for breakfast, but it was worth it.

Many a time, I lift up a thumb and index finger against a piece of clothing and I say to Mary, 'Mary, who owns these?' and we always fall about laughing.

We headed out the road following the direction the hostess described as 'bonito' as we waved our goodbyes. She meant the road was pretty, which it was, but another description would have been more useful. We rounded the first corner and were met by the largest staircase I had ever seen leading into the mountain and practically reaching the clouds. It was so steep the bikes wouldn't get past the first step. There was no hope of us getting up there without killing ourselves. I urged Mary to pray for an angel.

The prayers were said as we looked in wonder at the huge steps. I thought of John of the Cross who spoke about prayer and hope. He said that, 'In all our necessities, trials, and difficulties, there is no better or safer aid existing for us than prayer and hope.' Immediately, two young men appeared and showed us where the road was that saved us from having to climb the staircase.

Every new day should start with a prayer for guidance, and every saint and scholar was summoned to keep a good watch on us. The road started with big climbs that went up and up and up. The sweat was running and my heart started to pound so much I though the birds could surely hear it. After an hour we settled using the gears well, standing out of the bike for balance and to rest the legs. There were 10 per cent and 12 per cent hills going upwards and it was almost impossible with the amount of things we had in the bags. I thought of Jesus carrying the cross, shouldering our burdens, asking us to love and help one another.

A crowd of us ended up outside a restaurant that evening waiting for it to open at 9 p.m. The cheese and onion sandwich we had eaten earlier did little to replenish the energy used that day. We lay down to sleep by 11 p.m. on the usual offering of a crowded room of bunk beds. There was a melody of snoring in the room that even my ear plugs couldn't mute. It would be a long night. A fly kept landing on my bed, buzzing in my ear, and I thought how the devil came in many forms. When I eventually got to sleep my dreams were full of soldiers in chariots, pulled by magnificent horses. I was reminded of Dr Brian Weiss and his books full of wisdom. He spoke about hypnosis and putting the person in a state that holds great potential for healing (a magical forest that holds the healing tree). Each night I was in the magical forest and I was eating the sacred berries of the magical tree. There are no boundaries in the subconscious mind and I was in deep awareness of all I was seeing and living through at night. This one had taken its toll on me, leaving me tired, and wanting time to recall and learn from the memories.

Glancing in the mirror I hardly recognised myself. I looked so drawn and tired. I moved like a robot in slow motion. It was hard to keep up with Mary, who was already tucking into coffee and biscuits for breakfast, hardly a substantial meal considering what was in front of us. The mist drifted down the mountain as thick as clouds, and we could hardly see our hands in front of us as we moved out onto the road. We tied our raincoats around our heads and pushed the bikes in front of us with our heads down to avoid the blinding rain. The mist got thicker and the rain got harder, and on and on we climbed, up into the sky.

After about six kilometres of sheer climbing we found a shop and stopped for coffee and a cheese and tomato sandwich. The sign above the door read 'Eliza' and Mary took a picture of it.

'Another person from the bible to acknowledge en route,' I said.

Mary shook her head and said, 'I think this is about you, Elizabeth.'

'Me? Why me? What do you mean, Mary? It's the angels,' I replied. 'They are giving us signs to follow.'

The rain continued as we continued our ascent on foot. The slippery surface made it unsafe. From deep within the mist beside us we could hear the roar of cars and lorries as they passed us by. It was frightening. St John of the Cross was telling us to slow up, be safe and enjoy the moment and not to rush the Camino. There was a pounding of ghostly footsteps and I felt my dream was becoming a reality and the chariots were after us. When the mist eventually lifted the scenery was breathtaking and the smell of the soaking grass was hypnotic. We stood to the side as if to make room for the pounding footsteps of the past. For centuries, generations of people have tramped these roads; it would be hard to miss their presence. A yellow arrow appeared out of the mist and we cheered, pointing to it with childish excitement. We hugged each other in relief and posed for selfies!

The rain had caused the butterflies to shelter and I missed them. I asked for a sign from the angels, and they responded when a leaf slowly dropped off a tree and danced in the rain. There are many ways the angels let us know that they are around, we just have to keep watching and asking when we feel the need. A fork in the road appeared and decisions had to be made, when out of nowhere a butterfly appeared. It was the red admiral, the leader of all butterflies, letting us know it was the right pass to follow. We smiled at each other in understanding and acknowledged the butterfly with a nod.

What goes up must come down! We had been climbing for a long time without looking at the time, and the backs of our legs were letting us know they needed a break. The descent came quick, like everything else in life, and we hadn't even time to think of the danger or what lay ahead. The pressure holding the bike backwards to keep it from swaying caused my hands to go numb. It was worse than going up, as there would be nothing we could do if we hit a stone, a sheep, or even a donkey on the way down. We were at the mercy of the Lord and St Michael was called upon to guide us down safely. After a few hours we came to a narrow cobblestone road. It was truly ancient. Exhausted and hungry we asked some pilgrims if they knew of an albergue nearby. We were standing beside a narrow gate above a stairway. A man pointed to the stairway and realisation hit me; the struggle was not over yet. We had to go down at least fifty steps to get to the albergue. Looking at the distance and the bikes, simultaneously and almost in silence we took the bags off the bikes and walked down carrying the bags one at a time. Laughter was far away, as we needed every ounce of energy to concentrate on the steps. A high wall of old sandstone hid the building behind. Bushes and roses grew along the wall. When we turned the corner we saw the doorway only 200 metres away.

Thrilled, we entered the gate and found an eleventh-century building, a convent. We were met by a nun who led us inside. She was from an enclosed order. The rooms were actually in an old church that had been made into accommodation for pilgrims. It cost €10 for the night and it had a peaceful feeling about it. She showed us to our beds and told us where the shower was. She moved silently like a ghost in the night, leaving us to explore the surroundings ourselves. We were both awestruck at the find, and with our spirits lifted we began to unpack. That evening, when we found a place to eat in Laredo, I devoured my dinner like I hadn't eaten in a month. I was grateful for the hot food, as we had survived on sandwiches for a couple of days. Mary spotted a hairdressers and decided to get her hair cut, only to realise she had forgotten her purse at the restaurant. Exhaustion was taking its toll; she had almost forgotten her coat on the bench earlier that day, and I had left my T-shirt behind at the previous accommodation. Thankfully, the girl at the restaurant was waiting for Mary to return and she handed her her purse and passport.

I knew I would have a peaceful sleep that night in our Franciscan convent amongst the order of the Poor Clare's. St Clare was an Italian saint, one of the first followers of St Francis of Assisi. Like him, she loved nature and animals. I closed my eyes, thinking how all roads lead to Santiago, regardless of where you come from. You meet people for unknown reasons that may help you change your life, or you might help change theirs, or indeed we might change our own. Nothing would be the same after Santiago; I just knew it.

At 6.30 a.m. the nun turned on the light and walked away without saying a word. People began to rise and move around, gathering their things. Mary said she thought we should stay another night and rest, and look about this historical old village. She had heard a voice telling her all night to stay and rest. I was happy the plan had been set while I slept. I believed St Michael and St Gabriel had communicated through Mary as she slept. They knew we needed to rest and there was more for us to see of the historical town, which was important for our cultural visit and education. A Camino is all about education and learning about each other, our similarities and our differences.

We were sauntering up the street with the sun on our faces. There was a fresh breeze shaking the trees, stirring shadows on the path. They looked like dancing angels. We met the large group of German pilgrims again. They were having lunch in the village and they called us over. There was a sense of delight as we shook hands and sat beside them. We had met them the first night in Orio, in the house on the top of the mountain called St Martin where the teenagers had given us their bed. One member of the group had hurt her ankle. It was badly swollen and I told her to put ice packs on it and wrap it up. They were contemplating what to do if she could not finish the trip. Stirring her coffee and looking thoughtful, the young girl said, 'I will go by bus and meet you at the finishing point each day until I am able to walk. That way we can all finish in Santiago together.'

'A good idea' said her brother, as he kissed her forehead and pulled on her pigtails, causing her to laugh and playfully raise her hand as though to slap him.

Mary and I found the old city and the oldest church in the village: Santa Maria the Assumption. It was a most interesting place, built on the land in the tenth century, way before St Teresa of Avila who lived in the sixteenth century or St Clare in the twelfth century. The amount of people who had gone before us was getting larger by the minute. Every one of them on the same journey as us, praying for intentions and asking for God's love and help from the angels. Their intentions at that time were similar to ours: a safe journey and a bed for the night, food for the day and directions for the next part of the Camino. I was humbled as tears welled up in my eyes and a tight feeling crossed my chest, causing my heart to beat loudly. To think that I was able to see and admire all that history and walk in their footsteps astonished me. All the struggles I had with the sickness and the constant worry over my mother were behind me.

I remembered the days from when I was nine years old sitting in the graveyard looking for her and all the time she was right there with me, leading the way. I realised worry does no good, as whatever is planned by the higher power is out of our hands. I believe people who have been spared sickness and tragedy have a duty to help others overcome theirs while they can. God grants blessings when we pray and we must honour his graces in return. Helping others is part of the deal, like all the people living around the Camino roads. They wait to do God's work, keeping the pilgrims safe; in return people pray for their intentions. The Camino could be anywhere there are people and a spiritual presence, therefore we should be helping each other every day and accepting the help gracefully as it comes our way, working together to make a peaceful world. That's my thought on life's journey.

We returned to the convent. The gentle nuns had allowed us to stay another night, which was not common practice, so we were grateful. The place felt calm. It was the silence. It felt like a safe place where one could lie down, drop the 'baggage' and feel enlightened from the inside out. It had all the signs that I had been there before and I had returned to remember a passive lifetime. I might have ended a past life there! What with Mary's dream, we both could have been there together! Who knows? There is so much we don't understand, and most likely never will about ourselves or the world we live in.

CHAPTER SIXTEEN

Nothing and No One Lasts Forever

'If you knew who walked beside you at all times, on the path that you have chosen, you could never experience fear or doubt again.'

— DR WAYNE W. DYER

We had stopped for a break and were sitting on a bench overlooking the sea. It was warm and I was glad of my cap. I looked longingly at the bright blue ocean. There was a shore of dancing angels in the sunlight, moving around skimming the water. I was mesmerised. Mary nodded off on the bench beside me. I sat and looked at the sea, watching the children playing about in the water. The beach had rough sand and it was surrounded by undulating mountains.

I closed my eyes and was transported back to when I was seven years old and introduced to the sea. A lot of major things happened during my seventh summer. My uncle Bobby and aunt Agnes, who had no children of their own, wanted me to stay with them in a place called Linwood. It was far away from our house and had very few houses around. There were no tenements with big exciting backyards to play in, no high walls to climb up and watch the moon and the stars. The first time I went I was picked up and brought on a train to the seaside. The train journey made me feel ill.

I was to be introduced to the ocean and the miles of water that had no end. I stood with my feet in the ocean and watched in wonder and tried to imagine the amount of rain it must have taken to produce that amount of water. I paddled and made up my mind that someday I would swim in the ocean. I spent weeks going to the seaside until I overheard something about adoption being talked about. I knew it wasn't good and I began to fret about not getting home.

I was happy enough in the daytime, when the sun was up and all the children were out playing together. One morning I came out to find a majestic field of golden daffodils;, bobbing their heads in the sunlight. I had never seen flowers in abundance before and the beautiful field of golden heads bobbing would stay with me forever as they are my most loved flower even today. But the night brought nightmares. I would lie awake afraid to sleep and wonder why I had been sent away. Had I not been helpful enough? Was I not wanted? Would I end up dead? I was away and that was my perception of death – to go away and not come back. If I was dead and in someone else's house, perhaps my mother and my sisters were also in someone else's house and not able to come home? My thoughts would multiply and my imagination ran riot. I missed my family. I worried about my aunt, my brothers and sister. One night when I was feeling so bad the voice said 'cry out loud'. I had been internally crying without tears. Once I started I cried all night and there was no consoling me. I wanted to go home and I did not care about the ocean or the daffodils.

The next day I was brought home and I made up my mind to always be good, just in case I was sent away again. I am entirely grateful to have had that chance to see the ocean and the daffodils, for my love of both still stand. I became a full time 'watch dog', trying to do everything good so my father would be happy. I hated my father for even thinking about giving me away. I remember becoming so quiet because I thought I was making too much noise and that's why he sent me away. I played silently after that and just watched what was happening. I could not understand why it was me he was sending away and I wondered and wondered if my sisters were living in someone else's home and were adopted. If so, who would be next? Life was so confusing and people were so unpredictable it was hard to understand.

Children need someone to chat to, especially in circumstances like that. I always chatted to the angels. I had a scrapbook full of them. There were large and small ones with magnificent wingspans and beautiful colours. I would sit and stare at them and wonder at their existence. Did they all live in heaven, or were some of them here on this earth? Once, while standing on a chair in my grandmother's kitchen and looking out the window at the rain and the stray black cat sheltering under the hedge, I inquired about the whereabouts of the angels.

'Angels are in the sky in the form of the stars,' she replied.

From then on I would lie on the ground and look up at the clouds waiting for the stars to appear. I counted the angels till I got dizzy.

My grandmother also told me there were 'earth angels' that looked after people. Earth angels were people who helped others with their shopping, their children and old people, including doctors and nurses who helped to heal people. I wanted to be an earth angel, and I made up my mind to help people by doing a good deed, like shopping and housework. Every chance I got I would ask to help. She also told me we all have a guardian angel, sent from God to walk by our sides, and we could call on them any time we needed help if we were afraid. This was powerful information and I began to tell my friends about our guardian angels and it wasn't long before we were all talking about them. That kind of childlike chatter makes the angels happy and when we talk to them we begin to see signs that they are around, like the butterfly or the white feather that is said to be a message from St Michael the Archangel, God's right-hand man. I wanted to know more about all the angels that are all around the Camino. So many saints walked and are still present on the Camino. It is so uplifting to imagine the help we can have on a daily basis, if we just acknowledge them.

Santander, the capital city of the Cantabria region, was the next port of call. This beautiful resort is home to the Cathedral de Santander with its octagonal cupola and Gothic cloister. A large boat brought people over in the morning to the road joining the Camino. It looked a bit out of the way and across the deep sand and I knew it wasn't going to be easy getting to the boat. The timetable said there were boats all day every hour. We were planning to go the next morning. Mary insisted on taking the eight o'clock boat, despite me voicing concerns that I thought the earlier was at 9.15 a.m. on Sundays. We hastily flew down the coast road only to find that I had been right. Others had made the same mistake and were clearly tired and annoyed with this delay. Nobody was very chatty, but everyone brightened up once the sun came out and warmed us up a little.

There were a number of young people from different parts of the world, including Lucy and her boyfriend. She was about twenty, was from England and studying Spanish in Edinburgh, Scotland. She had two ponytails in her hair. Her eyes held a pain that was clearly visible. Lucy was doing the Camino in memory of her mother, who had recently died of breast cancer. It was her first cycle. She was wearing her mother's shoes and her father's yellow raincoat with her mother's wedding ring around her neck. Lucy had no helmet and I advised her to get one. I gave her a picture of Archangel Michael and told her to ask for his help should she need it. When she said she wasn't Catholic, I told Lucy that God sent St Michael into the world to look after everyone, regardless of race, gender or religion, and that she needed to call him and ask for his help. I told her the angels are there for everyone. She thanked and hugged me and put it in her breast pocket. Lucy was clearly in shock at the loss of her mother; her sadness made her pedal the bike with passion. I hoped that the Camino would help her come to terms with this loss, and that she would learn to charge forward with her life and always look to her mother for guidance. I told her my mother was always there to be called and that I was doing my cycle for breast cancer research, and I was a survivor of both. There is never a right time to lose your mother, or your father, or brother or sister or anyone else you love. But it will happen, and when it does, it doesn't matter what age you are, it will still hurt and the unimaginable pain will rock your soul and crack your heart, leaving it fragile. My friend Vinney was hurting so much from the loss of his beloved wife it sent him to an early grave. His children had to get over the shock of losing both parents within a year – heartache that I believe could last a lifetime if they didn't learn to let it out.

The one thing I have learned in this life is that it's not brave to hide the pain and shield the sorrow. We should acknowledge and understand that everyone's pain is personal and we deal with it differently. But no one wants to prolong it, and people move on, but if it is still lingering and causing stress for a long time, then perhaps it is time to get some professional help to understand the healing process.

Watching my father hide his pain behind his half-mast flag of sorrow, breaking everyone's heart in the process, was heart-wrenching and in my eyes sinful and cruel at the time to his children. Through his ignorance and lack of feeling for others, death for us children became something to fear. Every day till I was nine years old was spent watching for him and my aunt to come home, and I followed my sister and brother around just in case they went away. My father hid his pain by drinking and smoking himself to death. In doing this he missed out on his life's purpose and all the joy one gets by simply being around children; children give out unconditional love.

A teacher once told me that time was precious and to waste it was almost sinful; it is something you can't get back. How right was she? Time is flying quicker than we can imagine, and we are getting closer to going behind the mirror than we think! Soon to be back with our loved ones at the summit. What do we want to tell them when we arrive? Do we want to say, 'I cried for all the years I had left and wasted my gift of life', or would it be better to say, 'I missed you, but I wanted to make it easy for you to be happy to rest in peace, by seeing my happiness and gratitude for my life and how I kept the lamp lit, by moving on bravely'?

While we are missing the people we loved we should still be living our own life, without guilt. Tuning into the conscious voice that never leaves us is vital at this time. Opening the flood gates is also important as to bury the tears will fill us with unshed emotion in the form of 'baggage', causing us to drown in sorrow that can make us sick. Lucy had a long way to go in her recovery, and we added her to the list of prayers, and wished her a 'Buen Camino'.

Having a spirit guide like your mother is very comforting. It can help people by being able to pray and talk to them and ask for guidance about situations in their life. I have always been guided by my mother, and I have asked for her help in all my ups and downs during my life. Out of sight doesn't mean out of mind; just because you can't 'see' that person does not mean they are not around. They are just behind the 'mirror,' watching out for you! It's a great honour to be able to acknowledge one's family who have left this world. Knowing they are around is very reassuring especially when one is sick or worried about a situation.

To believe and to feel the presence of a passed loved one is a constant gift we must cherish and not let grief rob it leaving us empty and lonely. One can get 'stuck' on the 'crossroads' on their Camino and not move on until it is too late. That's my analogy of my mother's untimely departure from this world. Death comes in the night like a storm in a forest. When she died the largest tree – 'the mother tree' – was uprooted and the young ones were left hanging in limbo, broken branches scattering the bird's nest and the young vulnerable nestlings were unprotected. My father was like a swan in a lake; when one is parted the other grieves for eternity.

Some young children can see or hear the angels and can follow instruction. I have always heard the voice of my angel. It has led me through so many trials and tribulations on this Camino. And I am entirely grateful for each and every one. Hearing a voice is one thing but seeing the person is entirely different. Many times in my life when I was in 'turmoil' and unsure of what to do next, my mother would sit beside me. Her presence was as plain to me as anyone else on this planet. She was the lady in the picture and I felt her love radiate towards my heart. At times like this I knew I was missing out on something extraordinary that could never be replaced. The most vivid time she made herself visible and sat on my bed was when I was about to give birth. I got a notion that if she could die having a baby, so could I. She told me not to fret, that she was with me and would be with my baby. I never worried after that.

We were 'robbed' of 'love' by losing our mother so young. This lack of love and direction in a young life can leave confusion and instil an emptiness that is indescribable. It's like a hole that can never be filled. I'm grateful for her presence and reassurances helping me love this Camino. For if I was to waste my precious time lurking in sadness, then her effort to bring me into the world would have been in vain, and it may have well been me that died with her. That's my belief ever since I could understand how she died.

There is so much to learn while we are here on earth and I don't want it to end anytime soon. I am grateful that I have had angels on my Camino, all through my life, and I hope they continue to guide me for a very long time yet. Perhaps other people will reflect and recognise their angels and the ways they communicate with them; listen and acknowledge their presence. Look for signs like the butterflies, white feathers, number sequences, people that come out of nowhere to help us. All of these are signs of angelic presence.

We should all try to be earth angels to others in whatever way we can. We may only see people for a short time; but in that time we may be able to make a difference to their lives. One small gesture of sincere caring and a few words of hope can save someone an eternity of pain. I hope Lucy can get some peace in her young life, and that she felt her mother's presence with her on the Camino while in Spain. I also hope that her experience continues at all other times in her life, no matter what country she is in. I know that by giving her the picture of Archangel Michael, she may feel him close to her and he can entice her mother to contact her. Feeling her presence will make all the difference to her recovery and someday she may do the same for someone else.

Archangel Michael needs to be acknowledged and recognised for the power he has to help people on their Camino. God gave us choice; we must choose to ask him for help, as he can't interfere in our choices. That day talking to Lucy had me thinking and helped me to open up the flag and have a good look at my life and what makes me tick so to speak. I realised all the running and wanting to see everything came from my desire to use up my time carefully, my need to do the best I could and learn whatever I could while I was alive. In a sense Lucy helped me uproot rotten foundations that were useless. Serving no purpose now in my life, they needed to be released in order for fresh healthy seeds to grow, to allow me freedom to continue this journey with a clean slate. Life is so wonderful, we should strive to enjoy every minute, even the hard ones, for they are what give us courage, hope and determination enhancing our trust in God.

Despite the beauty of the sea and the mountains surrounding us, I found it hard to enjoy them as I was feeling a little off-colour. I kept reminding myself how lucky I was to be on the trip and any hardship was only a trial of courage and determination. The wind was rising and the sea was getting rougher. I was sitting quietly, glad to be off the bike and have my feet on a hard surface. The boat was swaying slightly, but I was comfortable sitting there. It was then I truly realised that the Camino was for walking, and at a slow pace. We were going too fast on the bike to take in the energy and scenery around us. The movement of the boat began to churn up memories. They rose like sleeping ghosts, burning my eyes. I couldn't stop thinking of my father and I felt I was being unjust when I thought of him, because deep down I loved him. But when I thought back to some incidents that were arising in my heart, incidents that caused deep pain and confusion as a child, I felt burdened. Just as my bike was laden down with too much baggage, so too was I. Memories were being evoked and when I tried to push them back down I felt I would vomit. Trauma can burrow deep into the body, and it's a ticking bomb. The swaying of the boat seemed to free my mind and loosen my baggage, my memories.

CHAPTER SEVENTEEN

Baggage

'Sometimes things happen for reasons we will never understand,
Nor are we meant to: The plan was made way before we were even born.'

— ELIZABETH MCKENNA

The subconscious mind has the ability to store and recall information; our memories can sometimes be like 'hidden files'. Dr Brian Weiss explains that the subconscious has not been limited by our imposed boundaries such as logic, space and time; it can remember everything from any time and it can transmit creative solutions to our problems. The subconscious can transcend the ordinary to touch upon a wisdom that is far beyond our everyday capabilities. I believe I learned to tap into my subconscious mind and seek out guidance to help me get through the long confusing days of my early childhood. My dreams became like 'living events', so much so that I found it difficult to comprehend what was real. I learned when to speak and when to hide, when to stand and talk and when to run and hide. I also learned that every day contained something to be happy about and small things were always the best.

When I was young I would regularly pass a shop and talk to the shopkeeper, telling him about my day. I never failed to leave with a reward – an apple, pear or a cake – something to munch on as I skipped up the street. This reward kept me content and taught me that some people are kind and the simple things are the best. Other feelings of fear caused by wondering where my father was and what condition he was in were different and often caused me to vomit.

On the other hand the pleasures given by earth angels made life worth living. My father often became angry if we upset him; he would cause a fight and head out leaving us full sure we were to blame and I hated him then. I would run to a drain pipe, stand in the rain and feel the water wash away the confusion. I thought that God was crying when it rained and I loved to join him, for the world was a scary and confusing place to live in.

My father sometimes brought home men to play cards and drink in our house; they would land into our bedroom making the excuse they were lost, frightening us half to death. Shortly after my sisters went away I was sitting at the fire listening to my aunt Lilly sing her song about Galway Bay, with tears of longing running down her face. My father brought home a little black-and-white dog in a box. I trained her to sit at the door and watch out for the strangers. Men also lay drunk in doorways and if the lamplighter forgot to light the lamp or children put it out it would be dark and scary. Men were unpredictable and scary.

Looking back now, they were sad men. Some may have been in the war and some lost family and were suffering from trauma in the form of post-traumatic stress disorder. Some of these men would come out and talk to us and tell us to come into their house and we could have sweets. This happened many times to my friend and me. We went inside and sat talking and we would receive sweets and listen to their stories and head back out to play. One day, however, a man enticed us in to his flat. It was a creepy sort of place: dark, dusty and it smelled of beer and smoke. When we went inside he told us to take our clothes off and he would give us sweets. I began to panic and the inner voice told me to open the window and shout loudly. The window was old and heavy and yet it lifted as if made of paper. I believe my mother helped in the form of an angel looking after us that day! Around that time I became scared of all men, except God, the one I couldn't see, but I was full sure he could see me. God became the one man I wanted to know intimately.

When I was eight years old, my father fell from the rooftop in the big snow, breaking his legs. He sat in the chair and had to be helped to move about. This kept him from his usual routine and he had to stay indoors. I was so happy, not because he was injured but because I was able to spend time with him. I was glad he was home and so was my aunt; she became happy and sang when she was washing or cooking. I would run to the shop for his cigarettes and a bottle of beer and watch him read. Sitting together at the fireside, I watched his every move. I learned a lot about his ways and I saw another side of my father: he was fun. I loved this side of him. Although in pain, he seemed happier in himself, happier than I had ever seen him before. There was one thing I longed for and spoke many times about, and that was my mother. I fidgeted with her picture hoping he would see me and tell me her story. He pretended not to see this and kept reading his books. When I spoke he just changed the subject, and so I gave up trying. That time with him was short-lived but precious. He regained his strength and began to cook the dinner; he was a great cook when he was in his full senses. He cooked in the Royal Air Force (RAF) when he was a very young man at the end of the war. He could bake pies and tarts that smelled divine.

One day I watched him polish his shoes, put on his good suit and check his tie in the mirror, and I knew the good times were at an end. He headed out the door without batting an eyelid, and I knew sleep would be difficult that night. My aunt came home from work and I saw the sadness re-enter her eyes as she stared at the cold fire. She never sang again for a long time. From that day on one of my and my sister's chores was to go and fetch him, as he could hardly stand straight without his legs buckling under him. This was a scary job; he was so tall it was impossible to catch him if he fell over, and I began to hate once more. I prayed he might die and go away. I begged God to take him and send my mother back. My father changed once more into what I thought of then as a monster; he was selfish, demanding, argued with everyone. Soon my life was upended by him even further. As I slept soundly, I was woken by my father. The smell of smoke and alcohol was mingled with his slurred words. He took the liberty to see me as my mother. He used an excuse which he thought was 'okay' and that I would not question. He would tell me I looked like my mother and he wouldn't hurt me. My skin crawled with fear and disbelief and I knew he was lying. I was not like my mother. I was more like my grandmother, his mother. When these times took place I would pretend to be asleep and pray for courage and for someone to come home to help me.

One night I prayed and no one came and he wouldn't go away. Panic was taking place inside of me when my inner voice told me my body was the 'temple of the Holy Spirit' and I was to run and hide. I jumped and ran and hid under the coats in the hallway. I had memorised how many steps it would take and how high I had to jump to open the hall door in the dark, to reach the stairway. He called out for me to come back, and I told him I would tell. I'm not sure who I would have told, or what I would have said, for the vocabulary was far beyond my comprehension. But I knew it was wrong because the voice told me to run.

The understanding of that type of situation was way beyond my development at that tender age, an age when a child should be full of joy and contentment. I was building up fear and 'baggage' was forming and getting heavier by the day. It was the end of innocence and the beginning of disillusionment. It has to be the worst sin in the world to take a child's innocence and think you have a right, especially if you are their parent, one they are meant to trust. I wished he had died and not my mother and I continued to beg God to take him away and send her back.

I made so many promises to God and to the neighbours to help them clean the house, do shopping, wash the stairs and even stay away from the puddles of water, but it was to no avail, she never came back. From then on in, I would try to make sure I wasn't on my own and I stayed awake until he slept. I watched him sleep in the old brown armchair. I would catch the cigarette before it hit the floor for fear the house would burn down. One day a fire took hold, sending shocks through the veins of the whole house, burning everything in sight; stifling the life out of the soul of the house. Melted paint looked like skin that was charred and black. The curtains were misted over like a cloud had landed on them; the ceiling collapsed in various rooms, sending a cloud of dust up into the air, landing on every stick of furniture. Tediously it was put back together, but the lovely roses on the walls had died and they no longer danced when I approached them.

But I never gave up hope, and I prayed and asked God's help every day. Around that time we were being taught about Jesus's mother, Our Lady Queen of Heaven, Our Heavenly Mother. The hymns were so beautiful we sang them in the park after school. There would be a row of children on the rocky-boats and on the swings, with skipping ropes and bouncy balls, all singing, 'Oh Mary we crown thee with blossoms today, Queen of the Angels and Queen of the May.' I loved her. I had a mother in heaven and God the father and I felt blessed. I had another person to pray to and all the children loved to sing to her. It was a great feeling that would lift your spirits and keep you smiling even through a rough day in school. We were full sure she was with us all day.

As the boat rocked my memories, it was only inevitable that I would recall the long road to my granny's. Most Sundays were spent in my grandmother's house, after walking the long road of five miles. I always managed to fall in a puddle on the way up the road while trying to keep up with my father's long legs. He always seemed to be on a mission on that road. At times he would speed up and practically drag us and tell us to hurry. As I grew older I became aware of the section on the road this happened. It was when we passed the graveyard. I didn't know what a graveyard was for then, but I could always hear a voice calling me as I passed it by. I knew in my heart that it was my mother; it was the same voice that came in my sleep. One particular Sunday I asked my dad what was in behind the wall and he became agitated. He told us we could climb up the hill on the other side of the road, and he pulled at my hand to cross over. I realised that there was something I had to do by myself. I had to find out what was in there and why he never wanted to go inside. After that Sunday we walked on the opposite side of the road.

Another memory that rose to the forefront was the day I grew up and realised life was far crueller than one could imagine. I was nine years old and I had run home from school as normal to sit with my dog, who was called Sheila. She was sent to teach me about birth and death. The house was empty and I put my key in the lock. When I went over to Sheila, I witnessed the most magnificent of miracles. Five little pups appeared in front of my eyes. One by one their tiny bodies wiggled and jiggled into the world. I watched in amazement at the miracle of birth. There was a chill in the kitchen and I thought they were cold, so I gently lifted them up, placed them on newspapers in the old Victorian oven near the fire, which was flameless yet warm. The dog got out of her bed and she carried them back, one by one, to her basket. I marvelled at the way she fed them, and how they snuggled up beside her with their eyes closed. These puppies were to be my precious gems for a mere six weeks. I spent every waking moment with them. I never saw my father cry until one day one of the puppies got its head caught in a dog-food tin. I could hear it yelp as my father tried to wrench its head out of the tin. Thankfully it survived and I never saw my father cry in front of me again, until the day I left him for the last time. The puppies brought great joy to everyone, including my father.

When death comes it rocks the very soul. Skipping home from

school, my heart filled with joy at the prospects of a playful evening with the dogs, I turned the corner and was faced with smoke pouring from our kitchen window. My heart skipped and I thought it would burst as I climbed the stairs two at a time. I looked in horror at the fireman trying to give oxygen to a puppy. Another had the others in a bundle and said, 'Had they been a little older we might have saved them!' Another fireman came out the door with Sheila in his arms. She was limp and lifeless. At that moment I understood 'death' as being more than 'going away and not coming back'. I realised that to breathe was a gift, and without it nothing else mattered. I also grew up that day and realised life could be so confusing, cruel and frightening, and that not to pray could be a catastrophe, for terrible things happened even to those who prayed.

There was very little talk about the puppies afterwards, like they hadn't existed or mattered. I mourned silently in the dark lonely nights, under a drain pipe, in the church where the rain battered down against the beautiful stain glass windows, mixing my tears with God's. For I thought that the rain was God's way of showing us he cared. The accumulation of pain in my heart was tough for a nine-year-old to bear. Even today unleashing this memory brings pain.

I clutched my mother's picture, studied her image, her tiny smile and large eyes. Why wouldn't people talk about her? I now knew she was dead and to be dead meant to be gone forever. No amount of promises to God or good behaviour was going to bring her back, and my father was always going to be unhappy and he wasn't going away either. So I began to walk the long road to my granny's alone, stopping only at the graveyard. I knew in my heart she was there, and I began to search for her. I realised she had not chosen to go away and I wondered if my sisters were in that graveyard too. I spent many days and weeks looking at the headstones. I knew all the people there for I had learned to read their names and there was no sign of hers. I watched the burials; large boxes being lowered under the ground and so many people crying. I never found her and my father still refused to talk. Sometimes I would fall asleep on a certain tuft of wild flowers with sweet scent and I was sure I heard her voice. It was always calming and reassuring and many people stopped to ask why I was there. I placed wild flowers on graves where there were none. I continued this for a long time and tried to ask my dad to come with me, to no avail, and so I hated him even more. At that time I began to think that death was not that bad after all; one merely stopped breathing. I often thought that it might be better for me to stop breathing, to just die and go to my mother, for life was so full of confusion and so lonely. The only solace I found was in the church or standing in a puddle of water or under a drain pipe.

One day, I opened the hall door and I called to my aunt, 'There's a big girl at the door.' I didn't realise it, but it was my sister. She had come home. She was tall and beautiful and looked like the picture of my mother. A year later, my other sister returned. There was no talk about where they had been or why they hadn't come home before. The lack of openness and information and everyone returning to normal as if nobody had gone away was so confusing to me. They just slipped back into family life as if they had never been away. The adults probably thought this was the best way to deal with it. Meanwhile, my sisters would have been going through deep trauma, which was also hidden. They too were accumulating baggage that would haunt them throughout their lives – but that's their story.

God, I was getting tired of this boat, of the rocking, of the churning of memories. My brain was muddled and my stomach in turmoil. I yearned for dry land.

CHAPTER EIGHTEEN

It's Not Where We Are Going, But Where We Are Being Led

We got off the boat and reached the accommodation, which was close to the cathedral. It was a government-run facility, one room of bunk beds that held fifty people. There were spare mattresses placed between the beds for emergencies. It didn't open until 4 p.m. and when we arrived an hour earlier, there was already a crowd lined up against the wall. The young man in charge came outside, took one look at me and Mary, commented on how tired we looked and beckoned us in. Ignoring the queue, he picked up our bags and brought us to the large room, promising to get our bikes afterwards. He looked at a map of the room and led us to two single beds in the centre. Those two beds had pictures above them. Mary and I looked at them in astonishment. Above my bed was Elijah; Elijah of Tishbe is a person in the Abrahamic religions. His name means 'Yahweh is my God', and he was a prophet in Israel in the ninth century BC. Above Mary's bed was Our Lady of Mount Carmel, the patron of the Carmelite Order; Mary prayed her prayer into her mother's ear when she was dying. The goose pimples stood on my body like soldiers ready to march. There were fifty beds to choose from and he had brought us to the only two with holy pictures. I wondered if the message had anything to do with stepping into the unknown without fear. When we are at the end of our tether and not sure how to cope, especially when dealing with the death of a loved one or a serious illness, we can't give up hope. To give up hope is to be part of the walking dead. I felt my father was around that day and he was sending a message for me to try to understand. I believe when he was living he was part of the living dead, existing with a closed heart. Despite his fear of being hurt, he never stopped hurting himself till the day he died. God! It was as though he was saying the words and planting them in my brain.

Soon Mary and I were practically skipping up the street to enjoy the early evening. The seafront was full of people walking about market stalls selling all kinds of gadgets, including food and jewellery. We couldn't add one ounce to our baggage. A young French boy we had met previously on the Camino came over to us with his lovely Labrador. He sat down beside us, tiredness written on his face. It was the first time he had come across problems with accommodation. The albergue could not take dogs as it was government run. The bed and breakfasts could not take them either and the church refused him. I felt so sorry for him and we gave him some money to get food for himself and the dog. I thought it was a disgrace because dogs are pilgrims too; sometimes they are the only friends people have.

I woke refreshed after a peaceful sleep. I felt lighter in myself, like a weight had been lifted from my soul. I guess it was acknowledging my father. By 8.15 a.m. we were back on the road, wondering which direction to take. A middle-aged man pointed the way. He couldn't speak because he had had his voice box removed due to cancer. He was tall and slender with thinning hair and nice blue eyes and he reminded me of my father. There was a familiarity about him. He was a similar age to my dad when he died at fifty-five; he too had throat cancer. It was a terrible infliction and I believe it was caused from his lack of ability to talk about his pain and loss and the thousands of cigarettes he devoured trying to kill his confusion. I knew he was with me on the Camino and he knew I recognised him through the man's eyes. I felt him with me on the road the whole day, for his picture kept coming into my head, and I believe he was giving me encouragement and seeking forgiveness for all those disturbing memories that filled my mind.

We ate our breakfast at a lovely old church dedicated to St John of the Cross, who was also making his presence known throughout this trip. We were getting stronger and I felt better in myself. The climbs were high, but we managed them all. The butterflies were out in droves leading the way. It's a prodigious feeling watching them distracting us from the discomfort of the climbs. Yellow arrows and shells dotted the roads – symbols of achievement and security all wrapped up together.

A divide in the road left us unsure of the way. After a silent prayer to Archangel Michael, a man appeared to show the way. He looked like a mountain man on a mission. He had a long beard, was dressed for walking with a bag on his back and his deep-set blue eyes and ragged hair startled me. He moved like lightning, digging his stick into the ground up to the road above. It was a long climb up and difficult with the bikes. The muck stuck to my shoes and I slipped towards him as if on skates. He came down and began pushing Mary's bike up as if it was a feather, and Mary and I pushed mine. St Michael always comes to the rescue and never fails to know what is needed. We all stood studying a large map on a tree, and simultaneously jumped with joy when we saw the road. After wishing us a 'Buen Camino' he disappeared as fast as he had appeared.

My arms were tingling, my legs were in spasm and we were both starving as we came upon a canal that led into a town. I was wondering where we would lay our headd for the night and thinking it was about time we found somewhere. I offered a gentle reminder to St Michael that we were still in need of his guidance as it had been a long day. The sign said 'Santillana del Mar' with no distance marked. According to the map, the place was still a long way down the road. It was hot and we needed water. We turned a corner and landed straight in front of a water fountain that had a sign which read, 'Fuente del Peregrino'. That meant the water could be drunk and it was there for pilgrims. With our thirst quenched and bottles filled, we moved on slowly on tired legs. I spied a sign for an albergue to the right of a cornfield. We headed down with some excitement only to be met with a hill, which felt like a mountain. Every hill is like a mountain when one is pushing with tired legs. Climbing relentlessly, I began to think that at times small challenges in life can feel like they are too big to conquer, and we stop and don't move on for fear we won't make it to the finish. With this in mind, I hauled myself out of the saddle, dug deep and put every bit of energy into the last hurdle. We made it and were rewarded by a lovely welcome from a family on a farm. They sat around the tables in the large garden full of apple, lemon and lime trees and the smell of food was mouth-watering.

The lovely little lady in her sixties, with fair hair clipped back to the side and a floral dress, directed us to a seat. She poured us an ice-cold lemon drink, and we drank it as if someone would try to snatch it, such was our thirst. Content, I sat back and contemplated the day. It had been tough but once again we landed in a little piece of heaven managed by earth angels. They were friends of St James. These were very holy and spiritual people with statues everywhere, reminding people of all the help on offer here on earth. I could hear chimes blowing in the breeze, which reminded me of Margaret Solis telling me about St James, the Camino and that my father would also be with me. I decided right then to be open and to acknowledge him more on the Camino and in my life in general. I had shut him out and I would invite him back into my life and look at all the things I had learned from him, good and bad. I felt I was being challenged to seek understanding of life itself and my part in this life.

Having selected a room and taken a shower, we washed our clothes and hung them out on the line: two pair of black shorts, two cycling jerseys and two pair of white socks. That's all we used every day and yet the bike was heavy and felt like a donkey! Sitting down on a lovely garden seat we wrote in our diaries and ate fruit from the trees. Our exhaustion was forgotten. The view out over the fields was breathtaking: red stone slated roofs, piles of wild flowers, cattle grazing, and lots of butterflies dancing around us. We had made it another day safely to a superb destination.

The lady was a real mother figure. She busied herself, cleaning up and cooking dinner for everyone: pasta with pork and salad and a nice glass of wine to wash it down. I felt the lovely familiar feeling I had before in various places, including the Alhambra in Granada. That was like reliving a former lifetime and I knew where things were in that place even though I had not been there before. That's what I felt on the Camino. We decided to stay and see the historical town. The lady showed us the way, pointing down the road ahead of us, but all I could see was fields. She told us to turn at the bend. Of course Mary and I were chatting so much we missed the turn.

'God, but we get carried away in nature and cause ourselves more stress by not watching the signs,' I said to Mary, and we laughed and agreed we had been moving in the wrong direction.

Eventually we reached the historic town of Santillana del Mar and the ninth-century church that was hosting an exhibit dedicated to the freedom of women in Morocco. It told a story of very talented people, creative and yet so cruel to their own people and people from different countries: torture, rape, dictatorship and blaspheme. I wondered how this could still be going on in today's world where people are supposed to be 'educated'. I think as long as people live and are not satisfied in themselves, there will always be unrest in the world. If people showed as much love for fellow human beings as they do aggression, the world would be filled with happiness.

Strolling through the streets of the old town, all the ancient buildings left the mind open to imagination. I thought about people hanging on to the past so as not to forget their origins and what makes them who they are. There will always be an interest in the past; that is what makes it history. But should we live in the past and not move on and learn from the past? Wars happen because people don't move on; they simply want revenge. It is difficult to understand everything that happens, but I do believe things happen for a reason and Mary and I were led there for a purpose. There was a purpose to our journey because Mary and I never planned one day and if we tried to, it never worked out how we had imagined. As I said to Mary, 'It's not where we are going, but that we are being led.' I felt a strong presence in that town.

The Cathedral Colegiata De Santa Juliana stood in the centre of the town. As I sat in its cool comfort, I thought about the cruelty suffered by all the martyrs and saints during their time on earth, a cruelty that still persists and sometimes causes the alienation of people from the Church. Sadly, people have been scared by priests and nuns, making them stay away from churches. Those clergy were blaspheming God's name by their crimes against the young and vulnerable children. They also give a bad name to all the good true clergy who are following God's calling. This type of crime harbours feelings in the subconscious mind of the abused that can rise up to haunt them. People can feel so bad about themselves, the pain becomes internal and so unbearable they may think it better if they died. When I was a child and in that type of situation I often thought that was the solution for the guilt and pain I felt around my father and his abuse. I thought it was somehow my fault and I wanted to die. It was only through prayer and listening to the answers that I began to see it was no fault of mine.

Suicide is so prevalent today. People get so disheartened with all the trauma, wars and cruelty around the world coming into their homes from all types of media. Having a relationship with God at these times can help to bring people into the moment and take that split second off their pain to realise that this type of cruelty has been going on since before Jesus was crucified. The people who are walking the Camino today are not much different from when St James arrived in Spain to preach God's word. We are in search of solutions to life itself and that is only gained by living each day in some silence, making it possible to appreciate the heartbeat as a precious gift.

I was happy to leave the cathedral and get out into the fresh air. I felt satisfied with the day and was eagerly waiting the next part of the journey. For me the arrows and the shells bring us back to when we were kids on an adventure, or treasure trail, seeking a prize.

CHAPTER NINETEEN

A Camino Within a Camino

'Some roads are chosen and some are destiny.'

— ELIZABETH MCKENNA

My dream the previous night was more of a vision leading me on a long road; it was hot and I was looking for something when I came to a hill. There was a house with a lovely garden. There were four dogs barking; one was an Alsatian. I was walking towards the house and there was music playing and fruit trees hanging around the outside. A horse was grazing in the field. I woke and told Mary my dream. She had been dreaming of white horses. I felt the outcome and meaning would be revealed in the day to come.

Later on, we came across two nice young men from Lithuania. They were Jesuit brothers and had studied in Salamanca and in Ireland. They had stayed for a while in Gardiner Street Jesuit house in Dublin, and they knew my dearest friend Brother Eamon Davis. Brother Eamon was one of the first people I met when I came to Dublin. I asked him if he knew where there was a swimming pool and he brought me down to the one in Belvedere College, where he lived and worked. That was the start of a lifelong friendship, and a career for me in teaching people to swim, spanning forty years now. He is a wise and gentle man, and he told me that 'God wants us all to be happy' as he handed me a picture of the laughing Jesus. Every time I see that picture I realise that not only are we meant to feel sadness, but we should always feel glory and happiness, even in the darkest of days and nights when the storm on the inside is every bit as scary as the one on the outside. It's at times like that we should remember the rainbow after the storm is magical and beautiful, and we should always find something to laugh about and be grateful for.

I wanted to follow the arrows and Mary wanted to go right. We eventually followed the arrows and up the hill and over the bridge, and on the way down we came across a little church with a cross on top and white horses in the field. We realised this was the road in Mary's dream.

I wondered what the significance of the cross was. We had walked miles the day before without watching where we were going. Sometimes we were going miles to find what was already on our doorstep. Like Santiago and this beautiful church we were so anxious to see, when in reality we had seen so many, any of which could have been Santiago had we had a mishap.

We came upon the prehistoric Cave of Altamira. Some of the first writings ever found on the planet were in there. The trip through of the cave was like going back to the beginning of time and the beginning the Camino. Even though we were moving forward at a fast pace, the past was all around us and catching up with us. I had heard there is no going back on the Camino; we could look back and learn from the past and make decisions for the future. My mind was sending me back to revisit trying times in my life, particularly when I was a child. I comprehended I was to make a conclusion of some sort somewhere on this Camino.

The Altamira spreads inward throughout the entire cave until its final gallery, with more than thirty representations of animals, signs and various 'masks' shown in the Neocave's exit hall. It's a very worthwhile place to visit; it certainly sends the mind in turmoil and I acknowledged we all wore 'masks' in our lives to hide the hurt and the confusion of life itself, to hide the true being of the soul that is sheltered and hidden and afraid to shine.

Back outside in the blessed light, I opened up a map I had picked up in the church the previous day. It showed another Camino route: the route of the Holy Cross. El Camino de la Vera Cruz is situated in the region of Murcia. I got goose pimples reading it. The picture in my dream flashed across my mind of a cross on a church on a high hill. After reading some of the information about this Camino and the monastery, we looked at each other and nodded, both instantly knowing we would end up there. I placed the book in the bag thinking no more of it for it looked to be miles away and in the opposite direction to Santiago de Compostela.

Approaching an old run-down sign for an albergue at the bottom of a hill, I recognised it immediately from my dream. I told Mary and said that there would probably be four dogs and a horse up there. We didn't want to leave our bikes at the side of the road to go and find out if there were rooms, but we couldn't face bringing them up either. Just then a young girl in a car came down the hill and stopped and we asked if there was any room. She didn't know but offered to drive back up to find out for us. She returned with the great news that there were two beds available.

'They are for us,' I said as we struggled up the steep hill. I looked around and realised I had seen this place before and I could describe it intensely and accurately to Mary. It was the place of my dream the previous night. We saw three dogs on arrival and I wondered where the Alsatian was. A young man of twenty came out of the house with the Alsatian and welcomed us. I was astonished as it was so real and I even knew where the horses were kept. They were a lovely family and the young man was a fan of the Irish Rugby team, in particular Brian O' Driscoll. I was admiring the garden and the butterflies dancing around us as we sipped lemonade. I thanked God for being so good to us.

Sitting in the garden reading the map from the previous day, we noticed there were two distinct routes: one following yellow arrows and another following red arrows. The red arrows indicated the Camino of the Holy Cross, which derived its name from an old monastery along the route that held a relic of a small piece of the cross upon which Jesus died. It was called the Reliquia de la Santa Cruz. The fifth-century monastery was based in Santo Toribio de Liébana, just outside a place called Potes. There is also one of these crosses in Rome, Jerusalem, Santiago de Compostela and Caravaca de la Cruz in Murcia. We have since seen them all except Jerusalem. Perhaps that will be part of the Camino in the future?

After a peaceful sleep with no disturbances we gathered up our things and hauled them outside onto the path to get dressed so as not to disturb the other guests. There were clothes everywhere and we began to laugh. The bikes kept falling down, sliding onto the slippery tiles, and it took us about forty minutes to get everything together. The family had risen early to give us breakfast and see us off. Mary had opened the book in the morning at the page for the route of the Holy Cross Santo Toribio de Liébana. We decided that if we came by the signs for that route again, we would follow it, because the dreams led us to the accommodation and the crosses were everywhere. Heading into a place called Vincente, we met some of the other pilgrims we had been chatting to in Santander. They were heading to Santiago. They thought we were mad when we told them our plan.

There it was! The sign with the red arrows pointing to the left and the yellow one pointing to the right: two Caminos, one to Santiago de Compostela and the other one to Santo Toribio de Liébana. After some controversy around the journey to date, we decided the Holy Cross was the one we would follow and we filled the bags with bread and tomatoes, fruit and some nuts. We filled the water bottles with water with a spare one in our back pockets and off we set, into the unknown. The map signalled some very high mountains ahead, but that didn't deter us as we both felt fit and sure of our decision. We knew there was an albergue at the top of the mountain, and the whole route was to take three days in total, according to the map. Anything else would be provided by the universe and the earth angels waiting for us, of that I was sure.

We trusted in God and the angels and set out into the unknown. It was the unknown this time, for we were heading away from the sea and into the mountains. At first it was exciting and manageable. We very quickly realised we were heading into the largest mountains I had climbed since being in the Himalayas four years previously. It was hot. We met a farmer walking his cows, and we stopped to chat to him. We spoke about how St Francis of Assisi had walked this particular route. I felt safe knowing we had another saint to accompany us and help us along the way. St Francis' affinity to nature and animals is well known. He likened the sun and the moon to his father and mother. No doubt he found great joy travelling through these mountains surrounded by nature, and so would we.

'We can look out for more signs of St Francis en route,' said Mary.

'That's a plan. It will keep us focused,' I replied.

Having companions in the form of saints was reassuring. Not seeing someone doesn't mean they are not around us. Having seen so many signs including the animals gave us inspiration to name that day St Francis of Assisi's day. Little did we know that the peaks we were climbing were called the Picos di Europa, the peaks of Europe. Dismounting, we walked for hours, enthralled by the scale of the mountain and the sweet smell of grass in the air. Regardless of the difficulty, we were in good spirits and we marched on up. Mary began to wonder what we would see at the top of the mountain. I was trying to focus on being in the moment. At one point a butterfly landed on Mary's sleeve and stayed there long enough to be photographed. We agreed it was some form of a sign and we would pay attention and not miss others. We would continue to acknowledge all animals that day in honour of St Francis, including the bulls with the large horns in the fields we passed. All thoughts of Santiago had gone on the wayside, and we were clearly on a new adventure, far away from the sea.

Charging on all cylinders had us boiling over. We stopped at a very historical village called La Fuente, meaning the source of the mountain. Its water runs down from the melting snow on top of the mountain. La Fuente is built into the hollow of the mountains and we approached on foot. A fresh peaceful atmosphere awaited us and not a person in sight. The sounds of intermitted chirping of birds, in harmony with grazing horses and a fast flowing river running under a Roman bridge, caused a vibration and a choir of music, making me want to sing. We approached a Roman church called Iglesia Romanica: an oval-shaped, red stone building with a cross high up and a bell tower at the front with two bells. Six men were sitting like statues in a semi-circle, leaning forward resting on walking sticks; they looked as if they were guarding the church. They wore peaked caps and had dark glasses balancing on the ends of their noses. Cigarettes hung between their darkened fingers and the ash piled up under their feet. They barely moved on our approach, but they were surprised to see us. After some hesitation, we asked about the albergue, and after a moment of silence, one man wrote a number of a house on our paper and pointed ahead.

Hungry and thirsty, we arrived at a blue door. A woman in an apron with long dark hair and a cigarette in her hand opened the door and looked at us. Mary asked her for the albergue. She went inside and came out with a long key. We both looked at her as she pointed to a large house up the hill. When I asked if there was a shop or a restaurant nearby so we could get some food and water, she shook her head. There wasn't even food in the albergue. I had visions of us tearing at the sweet grass, such was our hunger. Thankfully a young girl came out of the house. She had some English and told us of a restaurant a further three

131

kilometres down the mountain. Her name was Nuria, and she turned out to be another earth angel, as she brought us there in her car.

When we arrived, a friendly middle-aged man with deep blue eyes and receding hair smiled at us. We asked for food and he produced sheets of cooked ribs, chicken legs, lettuce and onions from the garden with the clay still intact, tomatoes on the vine, a bottle of red wine, two bottles of water, some ice cream and bread and fruit juice for breakfast. He put the meat on a large, flat tray and the vegetables in a bag and charged €20 for the lot.

The mountains have a way of stirring up the soul and linking events in one's life together. I think all the mountains have that ability and the Peaks of Europa were no different. The landscape was breathtaking. There wasn't a soul in sight and we were surrounded by towering mountains with snow visible in the distance – a glorious wilderness that left our senses open and our awareness heightened. Golden eagles flew around the mountain, their long wings flapping, sending out vibrations of music as they made their way from one peak to another. The height of these mountains ranges up to 2.570 metres.

At one point, I said to Mary, 'Lie down flat. They may think we were meals on wheels.'

We ducked to the ground dropping the bikes onto the road in the process. This made us laugh loudly and they squawked louder and an echo could be heard all the way to Santiago. The peace was radiant and we closed our eyes and all I could hear was my heart beating. That wilderness brought me back to a time when I was fourteen and my name was pulled out of a hat. I was one of four girls picked to go on a school tour to Aviemore adventure centre, in the Highlands of Scotland, where we learned to camp outdoors, pitch tents, cook food on tiny stoves, climb mountains and perform mountain rescue. I wasn't afraid of heights and I was the one to go down the mountain strapped into the rescue board, enticed to do so by a chocolate bar. Adventure was being planted within me and I was in heaven. I learned about the outdoors in many ways, but the silence of the mountains captured my heart. The Cairngorm Mountains have glens as deep as craters in a volcano, and the roads are smooth and long. In every corner there is a lough of water, and when the sun shines there is none more beautiful. It was autumn when I went to Aviemore, and I was fourteen. I was besotted by the autumn colours: reds, oranges and yellows. There was magic in those mountains. The first time I saw Ben Nevis it was coated in snow and the sun shone so brightly. The colours of the landscape changed so rapidly it looked like the Arctic Ocean. It was there I had seen cyclists zoom down to the glen and I made my mind up to one day become one of them. I now know every corner of those mountains, and so does my bike.

My body was relaxed and rested and so we mounted the bikes and prepared ourselves for the descent. I knew it would be tricky, but was not prepared for the extent. This was the hairiest twist downwards I ever remember doing since the Himalayas. The hairpin bends were so tight we needed to almost stop to lean into them or we would have been on the wrong side of the road. It isn't easy going downhill at eighty kilometres an hour. I could smell the brake blocks as they complained about the abuse they were getting. I thanked God there were few cars on the road meeting us on the opposite side. Every sinew in my hands and in fact my whole body, were on fire trying to hold back the bike. This went on for what seemed like an eternity.

We descended into a beautiful place called La Hermida, where we saw a bar and albergue. Two tall men met us and without a word took our bikes and put them in a nearby shed. We threw ourselves on the beds and exclaimed our thanks to St Michael for getting us down safely. We rested and ate and went to explore the village. Mary was walking up the street like a lady, swinging her bag and her hair brushed back from her forehead. I noticed she had her pink shirt on inside out and I took a photo. We both laughed out loud, frightening a little black and white dog that was walking on the path; he took off in the opposite direction.

The road into the unknown can be better and more rewarding than the one you know. I knew that if we had seen the hairpin bends and the sharp corners and had an idea there was traffic on the way up, we would surely have asked St Michael for a van. I had an innate sense of joy within me causing my heart to beat loudly. There was a surprise waiting for us at the end. I just knew it. With this in mind, I closed my eyes and hoped for a peaceful sleep.

A bright, cool morning awaited us and the traffic was few and far between. The birds were singing in high-pitched voices and you could hear the owls in the background. There was something sweet in the air and I felt content. Our intention was to get to the next destination before the traffic piled up. I led the way on a good smooth surface. We were surrounded by undulating high walls of rock with grass and flowers coming out of the crevices. The feeling was hard to explain. It just opened my heart and I was filled with joy. Moving along, the mountains rose up above us, leaning close, almost closing at the road. A hint of a mist hung above, just enough to hide the peaks and allow the light to guide our way. I could hear the river flowing gently, sweet music enticing us to sing our song: 'Oh Mary we crown thee with blossoms today. Queen of the Angels and Queen of the May.'

We moved along like two warriors on a mission. The sweat was pumping as we struggled to climb with tired legs that hadn't recovered from the previous few days. I could once again hear the pounding of warriors' footsteps and I stood up out of the saddle and tried to outrun them. By half past eight, the smell of coffee enticed us into a small café. It was filled with drivers sitting at the bar and around tables having breakfast. We sat up beside them and shared a coffee and toast with honey from the mountains. 'Buen Camino,' they said, as they watched us leave, having offered us a lift in a lorry. The traffic became thicker and the road got wider, with a path for the bikes the rest of the way. When we arrived in the town of Potes, we locked our bikes to the railings beside the church and the post office. Inside the church, we found a museum that held old scriptures. Some of them were ancient, hundreds or indeed thousands of years old. We were enthralled by the history and excited to be only one step away from the finish line of this Holy Cross Camino. I was full sure we were being led by the saints and they were having as much fun as us. I still found it ironic that we should take the high road, away from the sea and our intended destination, because of a dream, some old papers and a red sign of the cross.

We felt a little despondent when we saw yet another climb ahead. But we knew we'd be okay. Up and up we went until we reached a monastery nestled in a hollow, surrounded by trees. There was a high cross. Suddenly, like a bolt of lightning it hit me and I realised what it was that motivated us; it was the crosses, for when we were tired we headed to the churches for rest, reassurance and gratitude for a safe journey. Wow! This cross was the one in my dream a few days before.

I remembered Easter Sunday 2006 when Vinney and I were struggling up the Himalayas.

That journey holds a lot of memories and taught me so much about people and myself. I had stood in wonder beside him, asking myself why I was doing that journey. Now I know it was all part of the Camino and God's plan. God gives us people in our lives to help us help each other and to make up for the ones we have lost. I realise now that having Vinney in my life, enticing me to do that cycle, was all part of the plan.

A picture of my father passed through my mind and I realised that some people get lost on the Camino. A tear came to my eye and I heard him say 'you're not letting me in'. He was right, I wasn't. I guess the memories were too painful; it was best to shut them down and bury them among the 'baggage'. I was doing what he did: living in denial, denial that that part of my life even existed. I immediately made up my mind that as memories arose, be they good or bad, I would acknowledge them and let them go. He needed acknowledgment and was asking for me to recognise his need, of that I was sure.

We arrived in Santo Toribio de Liébana, placed our bikes against the wall and circled the beautiful building. Inside was a chapel that housed the golden cross with a piece of the original cross that Jesus carried on his back. An image of Our Lady of the Angels, dating back from the sixteenth century, and the lying statue of Santo Toribio are kept in the Gospel apse. Another door called the 'forgiveness door' opens solemnly on the jubilee year every four years. 2010 was a jubilee year. I would walk through that door for my father, as I felt he was looking to me for forgiveness. There is no one perfect on this planet and we all do things that can hurt others, some intentional and some from sheer ignorance – that's what I thought he was saying. I walked with him through the holy door.

I felt exhilarated about that journey's end. It wasn't Santiago de Compostela, our chosen destiny. I wondered when reaching Santiago if I would feel what I was feeling at that moment. There is so much talk about Santiago and so much written about the elation one gets when they walk into the square. I felt that this Camino was truly the ultimate, for we were led there and there were only the two of us. My heart was singing and I felt Jesus was congratulating us for our effort and our trust that we would be minded on the unknown road. We never once felt any fear. Standing at the Holy Cross, I felt I was being rewarded for my patience and the struggle that was more difficult than normal because my body was still recovering from the shock of the cancer and its treatment. I felt alive, I felt minded and I felt challenged by the Almighty.

We made our way to the monastery of Santo Toribio. Founded by the Benedictines, it is now run by the Franciscans. Awaiting us inside was the sacred relic, thought to be the largest known piece of the True Cross (even larger than that in the Vatican) and which has been worshipped here since its arrival around the eighth century. It was closed when we arrived and we would have to wait two hours for it to open. Unfortunately, as usual we were starving, so when I saw a couple getting into a car I asked Mary to ask them to bring us to a campsite that I had seen halfway down the road, where they served dinner. They brought us down and we ate like queens. Then we walked back up to the monastery just in time for the doors to open.

There were a lot of people coming in buses and cars. We were the only two on bikes, and the only two that had crossed the mountains and completed the Camino of the Holy Cross. I stood watching everyone getting blessed. I kept cleaning my hands, making sure there was no oil on them. I couldn't take my eye off this beautiful cross, such was my elation. When my turn came to hold it, I felt God touch my heart, and I heard Him say, 'Run to me, my arms are open wide and I am waiting for you.' I thanked my father for telling me my mother wanted me to go to Mass and be a Catholic. For without that gift I would have been in hell most of my life, not knowing how to get out, of that I was sure. He didn't have to do that; after all he was Protestant and had no trust in God since my mother died and yet he kept his promise to her. That was one gift he gave me; it was the only one I needed at that time. I thanked him and God for the guidance which was bestowed on us, on that epic journey. A lady in the queue took my camera and took my picture. I was calling Mary but she never heard me, she was chatting in Spanish to a monk. That photo is one of my most treasured possessions because it tells the story of God leading us along this journey.

The bright, brown-eyed monk, who reminded me of the one in the Himalayas who led me into his humble home, smiled as he stamped our cards and wrote our certificates of indulgence. There were certificates for this Camino just as there are for the Camino de Santiago. I decided this one was for my father; his indulgence for his peace of mind, in order that he could rest in peace. I asked God to give him his pardon, for he had got lost on his Camino, and all the hate I had harboured unintentionally was doing me no good. I promised to let it go. The monk thought we were the first Irish people to do that Camino; he shook our hands, congratulated us and directed us to the accommodation for pilgrims built on the grounds. He invited us to Mass the next morning in their sacristy.

The next day was the feast day of St Clare of Assisi. We would pray for her in Mass that morning. I was a bit excited and nervous as we knocked on the door. We were led inside to the private quarters of the monks' praying sanctuary. It was peaceful and spiritual. I loved the singing and chanting. At one stage, Mary was saying the reading the monk said and I had to control my laughter. I thought she was going to say the whole Mass. They wished us a safe Camino and we headed to pack once again.

I had spent a large bit of the night contemplating the journey and comparing it with other journeys. I came to a conclusion that we were being taught a lesson on this one: we were carrying so much and to date we had used all the same clothes and had no problem washing or drying them. We always ended up with food and a bed, and then what was the use of the tent, and the boots, and the extra clothes, and the spare book? I just knew I wouldn't get time to read.

I decided the lesson was that the accumulation of so much 'baggage' on our 'life journey' was a mixture of material and emotional, and it was passed down from other people, in particular the emotional. This accumulation of 'baggage' holds us back and slows us down as we move through life. Through time this will get heavier, weighing us down, making us sick and afraid to move on fearlessly. There is a big world out there and if we don't move on fearlessly, then the following generations will do the same.

I thought of a lot of people, including my father, who I had strived to help since I was a child. It was taken for granted. There are many people who fail to show gratitude when being helped. Some people are happy complaining and not really interested in hearing the solution for problems, especially when I say pray for guidance. They still live in the 'poor me syndrome' and are happier in their misery because like my father it was God's fault. I realised we can do our best for people, but in reality we are all on our own Camino and must weather our own storms and take all the lessons from each day. My lesson was to drop the 'baggage' and let people weather their own storms in the future. Praying for people is of the utmost importance, but it is up to them in the long run how they go through their Camino. They have to use their own choice and make their own decisions without blaming the past generations or God for their 'baggage'.

I could hear my father talk to me very clearly. He knew I had finally forgiven him. My hate was ebbing away, and the last to leave was connected to the death of my aunt Lilly. The day she was buried opened a can of worms that spilled out leaving us more confused and I suppose mesmerised at finding the spot my mother was buried under. The very spot of grass with the wild flowers that smelled like perfume. I had sat on that spot as a child and heard her call me. For she was lonely and so was I.

For five years I never went back to Scotland to see him. I couldn't get over the shock of seeing Lilly's coffin go under that ground in the pelting rain, my feet almost sinking in the muck. I knew God shed so many tears for her because he was happy she would be with him on the summit, while we would live in loneliness without her. Two mothers had been taken by the time I was twenty-one, and I looked on in dismay as my father asked me why God took two women away from him. Even in her death it was all about him and his loss. I hated him then more than ever. I wondered what she was feeling, lying in that dark wooden box. At least she would have my mother for company.

Loving your children is essential, particularly in the time of grief and loss, and he failed us in sharing that grief not once but twice. Letting children make mistakes and learn lessons is necessary, but helping them recover is also essential. Like God himself, he watches us and allows us to go on and on sometimes in a circle. Like us on the Camino roads when we could not make up our minds which way to go next.

In that monastery, I knew that I had seen life as being full of wonder, adventure and excitement, despite the sadness and the trials. I also knew that without God and the angels, these adventures would never have happened. This Camino led to forgiveness and reflection. While looking at the Holy Cross in Santo Toribio de Liébana, I felt profound gratitude to have the voices of so many, including my mother, to protect and guide me. Now, I was to drop the 'baggage' every chance I got: acknowledge feelings and let them go in prayer.

CHAPTER TWENTY

From the True Cross to

Santiago

'Although I have been through all that I have, I do not regret the many hardships I met, because it was they who brought me to the place I wished to reach.'

— PAULO COELHO, *WARRIOR OF LIGHT*

After descending the mountains we returned to the road of the Camino de Santiago. Firstly, there was some shedding of baggage to be done, and I felt determined to lighten my physical load just as I had done with my emotional load. We flung our things into a box, sealed it up and posted it back to Ireland. A sense of euphoria ran through me. I knew the rest of the Camino would be smoother and yet just as challenging. A strange sense of lightness entered my heart like a weight had shifted.

Three more glorious days pedalling in a relaxed fashion allowed more memories to raise their heads looking to be acknowledged. Every time I saw something that reminded me of a stage in my life, some not so sweet, I let them rise. We greeted a couple of cyclists who we had met the previous week. The boys were speechless when we explained our motivation to take the high road and still be back on track to Santiago. The pelting rain led us to a lovely statue of Our Lady of Mount Carmel, a sign we were heading back to the sea.

Our spirits were free and our bodies acknowledged it. We were eating up the kilometres; it could also have been the altitude training. I knew Mary was feeling good and I knew she would want to go all day to get to Santiago, but I had made up my mind not to kill myself anymore and to finish the day before exhaustion set in. My prayers were answered in the form of Mary getting a puncture. Mary was raging. The fact that the bike had been fixed that morning left me with no doubt that St Michael himself had punctured it with his sword. This was to be our resting place, Ribadesella in Asturias. Moving about in the day not knowing what was next was like the agony after the ecstasy, one minute exhalation and the next who knows what or where we would end up – that was part of the journey into the unknown. Like life itself, one minute you are making plans and the next they are changed, and that my dears is why we must enjoy each moment God sends.

We ended up in a hotel that was built like a ship. All the parts of a ship had been placed together diligently. The owner smiled as we entered his gangway. It was like stepping into the past, everything shone like new. The smell of Brasso brought me back to my grandmother's kitchen on a Sunday afternoon when we children would sit, huddled together, rubbing her precious ornaments till they shone like gold. This old ship-house had stood for a hundred years. A sense of serenity ran through me; I just knew I would sleep.

We chatted with a local man called Michael. He had travelled to Ireland and loved it. Like us, he was hungry for more. We shared a drink and studied the map. He warned us of the narrow, rising, twisting road leading out of the town. There was no sign of a bike path. The traffic leaned to the right balancing on a tight edge; one slip and they were history. With this in mind we waved our goodbye and slipped into the bed to dream of sea voyages and past life revelations.

Almost immediately I was walking with an old monk wearing a long habit covering his head, and he looked very confused. He was walking on the road and there were cars all around him. He seemed to be lost. It was Brother Eamon from Belvedere College in Dublin. I called out to him to come off the road, that it was too dangerous. I met him first in 1975. He was a godsend to me at that time, becoming a true friend for life. He taught me so much about swimming, competition and teaching; I will always be indebted to him. We were all part of a club that still runs: St John Berchman's Lifesaving Club. Brother Eamon is a humble man and a true warrior of life that seeks no reward for all his hard work. He is a man of Jesus and I love him very much and have no hesitation to seek his advice on any aspect of life. I am truly blessed to have had him in my life all these years, and to have him on the Camino was just an added bonus. He was one of my past life comrades, of that I am sure.

We were in search of an old monastery we had read about, so declined a swim in Gijón for fear of arriving too late. The moment I set eyes on it I felt it was creepy. It was being used as a training centre for people with special needs by then. Then we found out it wasn't actually policy to let people sleep there, but they had seen the state of us on arrival and took pity. We were led to a dormitory In truth, we had hoped to recreate the magic of the other monastery, but that was not to be. There was no food available either, so we ate the remains of our supplies. I lay in the darkened room in the top bunk, when a young fella tried to get into the bed. It had been his bed the night before I think. I don't know who got the bigger shock, him or me. I swear the place was haunted. I could see a ghostly figure walking, cloak swinging, for most of the night. By 7 a.m. the next morning, I had hauled Mary out of bed and told her we were leaving.

Like two convicts we made a hasty retreat and gathered the bikes, stopping only to take a picture.

After about thirty kilometres it began to rain and we came across a very nice little Roman town called Aviles. There was a musician playing a violin and we stopped to listen. We seemed to be going around in circles again, trying to find the road, not sure which one we needed. Up and down and around the houses we went until at last we were on the right one, acknowledged by a yellow arrow, which lifted our spirits. Another epic ascent began and the traffic was overwhelming. When we stopped, a man came out of nowhere with his bike and immediately asked us to follow him. He said he was a friend of Santiago and his name was Josie. We just looked at one another and did what he said. I knew he was a nice person; he had an aura about him and a gentle smile. Josie said he constantly directed people on the Santiago journey.

We sat down at a locked gate for our picnic and realised the bottles were empty. We spotted a tap behind the gate, so we said a prayer someone would come along. The angels obliged, and a man came by shortly. He unlocked the gate and helped us fill our bottles. We just kept looking at him and thanking him. He bade us farewell and wished us a 'Buen Camino'. The road ahead was inclining and we decided to walk. It felt right putting my feet on the road especially as it was still the Roman Road and one could walk in synchronicity with the pounding of the footsteps and the echo from the soldiers, which by now were our comrades.

Up and down we went, on and off the bike, just enjoying the day with the sun beaming. At first we felt good, as it was quiet. There were butterflies dancing around us; they were like angels in flight, teasing us. The road seemed to get longer with every kilometre and that was a sign we were getting tired and we needed to think of accommodation. The albergue we came across was not for the faint-hearted. It was small and dilapidated, had one shower and a dribble of water coming out of the tap. The mattress was awful too. I felt we might be carried out by the bugs that danced around it.

Heading on up the road to a restaurant, we enquired about accommodation for pilgrims other than the albergue. The owner rang a house and said the lady would meet us at the corner of the road. It was like the secret service – the lady showed up and beckoned us to follow her to her house on a farm and a lovely comfortable room for €15 each; we accepted gracefully. Such nice people help out when they can, obviously not wanting the government knowing about their good deeds.

We were out and ready by 7 a.m. the next day. It was 16 August and the plan was to complete as many kilometres as possible before midday. We passed the Belgian man with his dog, who had his own little bag on his back and a Camino shell around his neck – a canine pilgrim. After a while, Mary was shouting at me from behind, asking me why I was walking. I seemed to be moving as if I was on a mission. I couldn't get back on the bike. I felt someone else was in charge; it was the Roman Road dictating to us again. Gijón was written in both directions. We were being led back up the path and were a bit confused to say the least.

The sea was on our right and the road was identical to the previous one. It was the bridge that looked the same; it even had the same number 13 on it; that's what made us stop so suddenly. I thought we were going backwards and I remembered you can't go back on the Camino, just as we can't go back in this life; we can look back and learn from our trials and tribulations and move on. I think there is a danger in trying to relive past experiences specially because they were so good and we want to feel this experience again. We don't want to relive the bad experiences, that's why they are stored and hidden under the rubble of unwanted 'baggage' good or bad we have to accept it and let it go. I made up my mind every day I had treatment for the cancer to acknowledge every session with gratitude and let it go. These experiences are there for a reason and I don't want to dwell on the reason. The Camino has taught me to enjoy every day, even the difficult ones. That road went up and down for another hour and it all looked the same. The smell of fresh coffee and toast made us stop. A nice middle-aged man named Santiago bought us coffee, shook our hands and wished us a 'Buen Camino'.

The heat was taking its toll, dehydration wasn't far away, and my hands stung with the pins and needles from the pressure on the bike. Thinking of Santiago de Compostela was all I could do to keep me motivated and moving on. We stopped at a very old church dedicated to St Michael. A little old man who looked like a Roman soldier had a key and opened it up for us. We sat in silence praying for our list of people while recharging the batteries.

We arrived at Asturias where the next stop was accessible by boat and we missed the last one. The other route was over a very high bridge that would have taken another hour to get to the top of, only to be stressed out with the hordes of traffic that sounded like a runway and there was no way I was going up there. St Michael was called and almost immediately out of nowhere a nice group of young people came over. Realising our predicament, they rang a friend who was a boatman. He arrived, smiled and hauled the bikes on board. He was our very own guide and a gentleman. He was very proud of his boat and he pointed out places of interest. It was a beautiful evening. The sun was still pounding on our faces despite it being 7.30 in the evening. I was exhausted. Looking and listening to the sea did nothing to inspire me. I was tired out. There was a festival on and it was difficult to get accommodation and the only albergue was full.

We headed to the church for a few prayers. I minded the bikes and asked St Michael for a bed, as we were desperate. Mary went on a search and a lady told her where there was a hotel. I had visions of us sleeping on the bench. There was already a queue for that albergue too and we had sent the tent home. Mary arrived back with a smile. She had acquired the last room at the inn. The room was lovely and the people were too; they even helped park the bikes safely. I relaxed in a bath as Mary prepared the tea of olives, cheese and bread with a glass of vino – a gift from the owners. It was a change for me to be resting first. Mary normally has a nap while I get unpacked and showered. I wasn't sure where she got the energy that day. Mine had run to the lowest point.

Switching on the TV dampened the spirits a little. There were fires in Galicia, where we were heading. Just for a few moments we almost got afraid. I had firm belief the fire would go out and not reach Santiago or meet us on the road, and with that in mind I drifted off to sleep.

The next day was 17 August, my birthday, and all I wished for was a safe journey with not too many twists and turns to encounter. How wrong can one be? We immediately took the wrong road and had to right ourselves. Then came so many lorries and strong winds that we had to dismount and push our bikes. Precious time was wasted. There were many roads heading to Santiago and it was difficult to get the correct one. Eventually, we stopped to have breakfast, only coffee and a cake, not a lot of food for burning energy. Later we found a shop and filled our bag with food for lunch and a small bottle of wine to celebrate my birthday. After another fifteen kilometres of undulating roads, it was so hot our tongues were sticking to our mouths and we ate lemons as if they were apples, causing us to screw up our faces and making us laugh, until we saw the climb ahead. The advantage of a climb is the lack of traffic and the joy the butterflies bring; they danced and kept us amused as we struggled. Weary, we came to what looked like a closed-up factory, shrouded with rubbish. Relaxing in the shade we set out our picnic and hung the clothes on the bikes to dry. Birthdays are great days to remind us to be grateful for life and another year. Every year brings us closer to the summit. I never learned an awful lot when I was in school; but one thing I do remember a teacher saying was that, 'Time is precious and we shouldn't waste it, every minute is a gift and we should use them wisely.' I guess birthdays are times when we should be grateful to our parents for life itself. I gave homage to my mother, thanking her for bringing me here and always being by my side, even if she was behind the mirror giving me signs to acknowledge her presence. Although I had very little time with her on this earth, I know some day we will be together and I hope it's her arms I run to at the end of the tunnel, when my time comes to go to the summit. I hope she is proud of me for I never waste time and I am always curious as to why we are here on the planet, what the lesson is that needs to be learned. I hope the Camino will answer that question one of these days. I also thanked my aunt for giving me her time and energy and most of all her love. The only thing I regret in this life is she never lived long enough for me to repay her. I promised I would bring her home to Ireland to rekindle her relationship with her family and I was denied the time to do that. Her time was up and her purpose was finished we when were reared. Her passing broke my heart in one sense and freed me from the constant thoughts of the whereabouts of my mother in another. That day is one of those days that never leaves you. Every piece is locked together like a jigsaw, and the final piece was forced into place, the day she died.

By 7 p.m. we landed exhausted in a place called Aberdein, a little village with one albergue. The warrior of light knows the value of persistence and of courage, and he knows how to lose. The albergue was full. The warrior knows when somebody wants something, and the whole universe conspires in their favour. The people conspired to our favour and in a friendly manner, realising we were tired, they directed us to the next village which was one kilometre away. Mary cycled ahead to acquire the room and I went to stamp the cards. I chatted for a while to the people behind the counter and they were listening intently about our experience on the Holy Cross Camino. I thanked them and pushed the bike up the last hill to hear Mary call out that she had found a room. Apparently, the young man took one look at her and let her in. It was a lovely simply decorated room. Mary was washed and in bed asleep before I got into the shower. When the warrior wins a battle he celebrates and food was on my mind as a celebration for that difficult but rewarding journey. There was no dinner till 9 p.m. and we were starving. After a bit of discussion we went down and devoured all the tapas at the counter.

Empathy for people is the way of God and forgiveness is the way of healing. In Tibetan culture they say we are our own healers. But for healing to occur we must first forgive the perpetrator and let go of the experience; to hold onto negative experiences is to die at the arm of the intruder. Some people, like my father, take the 'easy road' which requires subduing their emotions and carrying them as 'baggage' buried within the crevices of the body. That didn't seem anything like an easy road. On that evening of my birthday, however, I paid homage to both him and my mother. As I drifted off to sleep the dreams started again and I could hear the voice telling me to 'slow down' for the rest of the journey.

For the first time, I felt packing the bags was a chore in itself, even though we had very little with us by then. For the first time I actually dreaded the day ahead and I had to pray for courage, tolerance and patience. My body was tired from the lack of sleep and I guess the ordeal from the sickness was still harbouring inside. Mary was talking about so many things and places I was getting confused: swimming one minute, cycling to Córdoba and then Santiago and so many convents the next. My mind was not able for so much information. I decided that if it took another three days I wasn't concerned. I needed to slow up.

I was feeling so bad I had to make myself eat the breakfast of toast and coffee. Starting out, I took the pace and sat in front. I needed a slow pace because I actually felt like Santiago was too much bother and I wanted my own bed. I prayed and asked for patience and more stamina in order for me to recover from the previous few days' 'hard work'. That's what it was beginning to feel like – hard work. Every step brought up more 'baggage' in the form of thoughts around my dad and I wanted to bury them but it was too late, the flag had lifted and they were making their presence known. I wasn't happy with what I was thinking. I felt guilty because of the negativity around the feelings about him.

It was raining, large drops of rain belting off the ground, and I was glad, as it made it cooler and hid the tears that were rising inside me. I was unsure of the reason, but I felt God was crying soft large tears in solace with us; perhaps they were tears of gladness for our perseverance. We put our rain jackets on and seemed to freewheel for an hour, just what we needed, warming the muscles without too much strain. Analysing the map we realised we were finished with the mountains. We were glad in one sense and sorry in another. Although the mountains are challenging, they are rewarding with spectacular scenery and less heat. I observed the walkers going into the fields on another route, their sticks digging into the ground. They never failed to rouse my curiosity as to why they went on the Camino and what drove them on each day.

We met a twenty-year-old girl from Germany who was travelling on her own. She had a tent and not much money for food, so we handed her some. She hugged us and wished us a 'Buen Camino.' We were her angels for that day and I hope there were many more to follow, for she looked like she was on a mission of the soul and I hoped she would find it. Everyone we met, ourselves included was on an inner Camino. That much I was sure of.

Christopher Hansard in the *Tibetan Art of Living* wrote that 'the soul is the inner world of all people'. He explains our inner world as being 'who we really are'. The question he poses is: 'Are we happy in our inner world and is it the place we want to be?' Our inner world, 'our soul', holds the key to how we relate to the world around us. It guides us through each day, encouraging us to reach our full potential. Without an inner world that functions in an integrated way, we do not have a life, simply an experience of living, spattered by periods of unknowing, powerlessness with a sudden need for control. When life seems more difficult and more powerful than we do, the inner world needs healing. Most people spend their lives 'floating on top of their inner world', sublimely unconscious of just how unknowing and how lacking in personal empowerment they really are. Having the courage to explore within will help unleash the beauty that lies among the fear and anger. It will transcend the eternal light, which shines from within all human beings into the universe, unleashing endless possibilities.

My thought on that analogy is that at the core of our inner world beats an endless love that needs no language or intelligence to be understood; love lies in and speaks in a heartbeat. We must open our hearts to love, unleashing the heart that is ready to be humble. Humility is the foundation of generosity; a lack of attachments, pure love and not seeking reward are the keys to living a fruitful life.

I experienced love in the face of a beautiful, humble Tibetan monk. Standing, smiling in his orange robe and his woollen hat he welcomed us into his home high up in the mountains. Love shone directly from his eyes to ours, and it was a powerful moment that left a feeling in my heart that is hard to describe. I felt humbled, grateful and safe around him. Love shone from every part of his body. It surrounded him like a halo of light. He was wise and he had a power that is indescribable. He and his fellow monks used their power to spread love and acknowledge God in a very quiet way. This monk reminded me of the little nun in the convent of St Teresa of Jesus in Avila. They were from different religions but both radiated the same message. That message I believe is having God in one's life embedded in our consciousness which brings us unconditional love without fear of the unknown. When we are open and exposed to the universe in a place like the Himalayas or in the Pyrenees, we must be in the moment, fully conscious and listening to our inner world for guidance. Lack of consciousness can leave us fearful, missing out on self-knowledge and the greatest adventure that any person can undertake – 'the voyage within'. My self-knowledge was growing every day on the Camino, and at a fast pace.

My father became conscious before he died. I could see it in his eyes, and I felt it in his arms as he whispered he loved me and he was sorry before I left him for the very last time. I hadn't seen him for five years until I got word he was ill. I had been so traumatised by my aunt's death and the unveiling of my mother's whereabouts I stayed away. I blamed him and the other adults that were part of my childhood for keeping her a secret and denying us children some comfort and understanding about death, reassuring us it wasn't our fault she'd left. I sat in the shaded room on a lovely August day in 1982 and I held him close when I felt his bones and saw the look in his big blue eyes, through his tears. He tried to say he was sorry and he loved me. I felt my mother around and so did he. I saw it in his reaction and I know he was also listening to the voice within himself. He had found the key to unlock true consciousness and open his heart. But it was too late and I couldn't ask him the questions I so dearly wanted to. It was only while on the Camino that I received the answer. I believe it is better to unlock the door when one is very much alive, can truly listen to the heart and have compassion and respect for all living beings. It is sad to live in ignorance and only find the key on the way out, and waste a life wooing what can't be changed or someone who can't come back.

That's the thing, isn't it? Sometimes death comes and rocks the soul, leaving it vulnerable and shaky like a volcano, unpredictable. That's what he was, unpredictable, when we were young. I imagine his illness gave him time to contemplate his life. He couldn't smother the pain when it rose up from under the flag that was shut tight. There was no escape from his thoughts.

I hoped that sickness and the indulgence from the Holy Cross were enough to put him at rest.

All that suffering, all that pain, all that anguish was all in vain; what a waste of life.

The ancient church of St John the Hermit awaited us. Legend has it that as he was returning by sea from a pilgrimage to Jerusalem, his ship encountered a dangerous storm that threatened to sink it. After safely arriving in Spain, John sought a place of solitude where he could devote himself to contemplation. He may have founded the monastery of San Juan de Ortega, named after him. He erected a hermitage for himself at a forested site known as Ortega (the Spanish for nettle). This is situated on the pilgrim road to Santiago de Compostela. The key keeper, a little old man with a gaping gap in his teeth and a large smile reaching his eyes, was the person responsible for opening the church for the pilgrims passing through. He led us in telling us of the hermit story. The church was so beautiful, plain and simple with no riches except the stain glass windows that told the story of St John. This piece of history gave us time to rest and rejuvenate our spirits.

The butterflies were in abundance once again, causing me to jump with joy knowing that we were in good hands with another bit of history unfolded. St John was also reminding us that he was with us since Biarritz, in the church of John of the Light. I felt my father was still around and I wondered if he was angry with me. Maybe he was happy I was unravelling the tapestry that had locked him in for so long, driving us almost insane. At that time secrets were all part of families, where people were hidden away and trauma was just another part of life, which should be accepted without question. From my experience in dealing with the aftermath of our loss as children, forced upon me and my siblings due to the lack of acceptance from my father, I believe the cause was post-traumatic stress disorder. I'm glad my father was on the Camino with me and I hope he knows I hold no anger against him. The most difficult thing for me was trying to eradicate my aunt Lilly's funeral from my subconscious. If I think about it long enough, the memory is still intact. Perhaps that is why I had sore feet, perhaps the root of my sickness stemmed from that piece of 'baggage'. That was my question and I decided to lift the flag and relive the experience once more in order to eradicate it once and for all.

Content after a good day cycling, tiredness rocked my muscles. My mind cleared of strange thoughts. I remembered the voice saying to 'slow up' and I told Mary I'd had enough for the day. She was a bit disappointed as there was only fifty-five kilometres left to Santiago. That could be like 200 kilometres if there were any mishaps or complications to encounter, and it would wash me out, of that I was sure.

Just off the main route to Santiago, beside a huge roundabout with various roads leading to the famous city, we entered a quaint hotel. That roundabout reminded me of the one in Malaga that scared the wits out of us. A lovely middle-aged man, with deep blue eyes that were full of pain, came to meet us. Pain was visible in his slow walk and by the way he hung his shoulders as he moved towards us. He brought us to our room.

We sat around unpacking and discussing accommodation for the next night when a swarm of flies entered the window. We were fly swotting for ages. The more we exterminated the more they came at us. We were laughing and jumping as we swotted, banging off each other.

'We better get rid of them Mary, or they will eat us in the night,' I said as I made a swipe and hit Mary.

After ten minutes they all disappeared as if in a hurry. Were they telling us to slow up and have some fun? Mary tried to book accommodation on the phone for the next night in Santiago. I was sceptical as we still had a day's cycle to do, and anything could happen.

'We will be led there Mary, just like this one and the others,' I said, as I prepared for bed in the hope of a good sleep.

Mary opened her email. She had a message from her teenage grandson. He was praising her for the inspiration she was bestowing on him and the rest of the grandchildren. He finished with, 'I love you very much.' Mary cried and she said she couldn't remember anyone ever saying that to her in a very long time. I realised at that moment that we were all searching for love. Love is what we all need to survive.

At 7.30 a.m. the next morning, 19 August 2010, Mary and I prepared for the last leg of our journey to Santiago de Compostela. Standing on the cool tiled floor, packing the bags, we chatted with excitement about the day ahead. Mary opened a book and found there was an albergue in the monastery in Santiago run by the Franciscans. This news excited us and we hugged and jumped about like two kids, as it was the same order as the one on the route of the Holy Cross in Santo Toribio de Liébana in the mountains.

'Imagine Mary, St Francis turning up again after all he did to help us complete the route of the Holy Cross and obviously he reached Santiago in his day. Were we following him or was he following us is my question?'

My stomach was churning with excitement and I just knew they would have a bed for us. How could they not after all our toing and froing and going up the mountains instead of the sea? Would this be it, the ultimate challenge complete or were there more mishaps to encounter?

We practically skipped to breakfast where the coffee smelled like pure heaven and the toast tasted like sweet cake. We were ready to go on the last leg when the nice man came out and told us he had put a screw in Mary's bike, as it had been loose. He was leading us out the door and telling us to mind the roads and to take the right road to Santiago. He began to tell us about his daughter who had been killed on her bike while studying in London for a master's degree. His tears flowed freely, his shoulders drooped and shook with pain, and he seemed to slow up as his mind relived the event. He wanted to show us on the internet the write-up on his only daughter, who had been killed by a lorry. I told Mary that I didn't want to see it. It would make me think of my own daughters, who used bikes in London. Mary went inside while I stood with the bikes looking at the traffic and saying a prayer for him and his family. Deep-seated pain in his eyes and in his body was evident, and he needed to share it with someone.

Mary came out 'frizzled' and 'agitated'. It's not easy getting on the bike after hearing that news and heading into heavy traffic. We were both very upset for him and his family, causing us to pedal onto the road, as if on auto pilot. After about ten minutes I realised we had taken the wrong road off the roundabout. There was no sign of any other pilgrims, not even another bike. The wind was howling as the traffic sped by, lorry after lorry. I heard the voice in my head saying 'stop now' and I screamed at Mary behind me to stop. She pulled up immediately and nearly crashed into me. At that moment a big convoy of lorries passed us by, almost dragging us with it. We fought to stop ourselves from tumbling onto the road and being dragged under. We were extremely shaken up and I knew we had to get off that road. Archangel Michael had spoken once again.

We cycled on for another ten minutes until we came to a coffee shop. There was a white van parked outside. We looked at each other knowingly and without uttering a word we entered. A young woman behind the bar and a middle-aged man sipping his coffee and reading his paper looked at us. We ordered coffees and asked for directions for the correct road onto the Camino. At first they didn't seem to know what we were saying. We showed the map to the lady and the man looked across and realised what we were saying. He beckoned us to follow him outside, pointed to the van, hopped inside and made gestures for us to follow. We went hell for leather after him, forming a convoy. Coming to a stop at a bend in the road he got out and pointed to a road heading up a mountain to the left. We looked at the height of the climb knowing we had covered our distance and this was unnecessary and would most likely prevent us from reaching Santiago until very late. We stood making gestures at the bike and the van, and Mary trie her words of Spanish. The man lifted the bikes inside and we joined him. St Michael in the form of a van driver was looking after us once again.

He pulled up outside a shop on the official Camino road. There were pilgrims from all over the world heading to Santiago. He hugged us and wished us a 'Buen Camino' after lifting our bikes onto the road. We thanked him and hugged him, promising to light a candle for his intentions in the cathedral.

We walked and talked to people on the way in; all on a mission with the end almost in sight. During the last ten kilometres on a broken and bumpy road a strange feeling came over me as I heard the bells ring from the cathedral. In a type of 'disbelief' I acknowledged Margaret Solis. Her prediction had finally come true. I had reached Santiago to the bells of St James and my father was with me all the way. And there it was, the cathedral of Santiago de Compostela.

When we pushed opened the gates to the Franciscan monastery, we were met by a statue of St Francis with the birds flocking around him. He had crossed the route of the Holy Cross many centuries before us and stayed in Santo Toribio de Liébana in the mountains in Potes, and then onto Santiago. We had walked in the footsteps of the saints, and they were still with us in spirit. A glorious feeling came over me as I stood and waited for Mary. I had written a few words in my diary as I stood looking at his outstretched arms:

> Saint Francis stands silently and focuses his mind on God's work as the animals flock around him like disciples. The birds fly around his head, making a 'halo' catching the sunlight. They protect him as he feeds the little ones that land on his body, trusting him completely. His very presence reassures them that it is safe to fly freely throughout the world. Knowing God is with them. A flock of birds take flight; satisfied, confident and extremely happy in mind and soul, from the nurture gained from Saint Francis. He was chosen by God to be their guardian angel.

Just as the birds and the other animals trusted in St Francis for their safety, people have trusted in God and walked securely and freely throughout this world for millennia. Trouble comes when we don't trust in Him and get confused and insecure. I had asked Him, in fact begged Him, to look after us every day of the Camino. I realised this had been part of my ritual since I first became aware of Him when I was four years old. Although the journey was difficult, it wasn't impossible and we made it safely to the final destination.

When the nuns saw the stamp for the Holy Cross Camino in Santo Toribio de Liébana they were excited and inspired. 'A Camino within a Camino,' said one young nun. 'It is only fitting that you stay here for your last night to finish your Camino.'

She led us to a dormitory which was normally reserved for groups. We had the whole place to ourselves. After we had unpacked, we walked to the extraordinary main square, the Plaza del Obradoiro. There we chatted to other pilgrims, young and old, male and female. Some were going around in a daze, unsure how to react to the end of their journey. The inspiration one feels is personal and different for each pilgrim, depending on the motivation that inspired them to complete the challenge. People hugged each other, united in sharing love from their Camino.

There was a closing ceremony high up in the monastery led by a monk. The whole group of people from around the world participated. It was a beautiful unexpected finish for all. We sat in a circle in the large hall, surrounded by pictures and statues of saints including St Francis and St Clare. I watched people from all parts of the world smiling at each other. The monk began the Mass and one person from various countries read part of St John's Gospel in their own language. Mary read in English. It was a moving experience for us, as we had started the Camino with St John of the Light in Biarritz, and we were to be reminded of him en route in the hermit church with the beautiful windows telling his story. Watching Mary go up to read was very emotional. She stood on the step, and with her biblical knowledge, she portrayed the Gospel of St John. It was time for her to shine. She could very well have been the most 'mature' person to complete the Northern Camino, with me not far behind. We had been the only two Irish women, according to the monk, to have completed the Holy Cross Camino.

I had Santiago in my mind for a good many years, and I didn't know what to expect on arrival. I now realise that Santiago is a place of congregation for people, like the Potala in Tibet or the Taj Mahal in

India – any place of a spiritual nature, where there is a feeling of peace, love and God's presence. All these people were on a mission, trying to comprehend the mystery of life itself. My journey on the Camino left me believing that life is everlasting and we are here to learn lessons. One of my lessons was about love and forgiveness. My father was my teacher for both of these lessons, and my mother, because of her absence, taught me that time is precious and goes quickly so should be valued and not wasted.

By the time we headed to bed, I felt I was sleepwalking and my brain was muddled. There was soft music playing in the night. It gave a sense of serenity and kept people in the moment. I was deep in a peaceful sleep when Mary began to have hallucinations; and that was that, she wanted me to get up and look about. I was so tired I could hardly move. I was concentrating on my breathing and feeling content when a man came in and called us to get up. It was 7.30 a.m. on 20 August. Everyone had to leave by eight o'clock. As usual, we were the last to leave.

As we stood in the queue waiting to collect our certificates of indulgence and stamp our cards for the last time, we watched thousands of people from around the world scurrying about like headless chickens and unsure what to do next. Some sat in the square clearly exhausted, rubbing their feet and checking their blisters, while others danced with joy. Music came out of speakers surrounding the square, and the nuns were singing praise. It was a great privilege watching these people, these pilgrims with their personal missions. The heat was stifling, and we were getting dehydrated just standing in the queue. But we were happy. When we eventually held our certificates, Mary and I hugged and said, 'Buen Camino'. It was like getting a degree, only more challenging, physically, spiritually and mentally. By the time we entered the church it was full, and we just managed to acquire a seat. A special Mass was attended by the people, bishops, priests, the young helpers, ushers and musicians. They all sang like angels, glorifying each other and praising the Lord for all the help. The smell of incense swinging back and forth from the ceiling in the giant incense bowl was hypnotic. I felt I was in heaven with all the challenges tucked away in my memory.

Sitting in the square surrounded by people, my muscles said 'no more Caminos' and my heart said 'just one more'. We looked at the map and studied the route to Finisterre. We thought of the glorious swim that awaited us there. The end of the earth was calling us! In traditional times, after reaching Santiago, people walked to Finisterre and burned their clothes there. They also dipped in the sea, leaving them as clean as the day they were born. I was exhausted and couldn't go one more step; either on the bike or by foot. I needed to go home to roost. After some discussion, it was decided we would do 'one more Camino' – we would walk from Santiago to Finisterre. I had visions of me being the donkey and literally carrying the 'baggage'.

CHAPTER TWENTY-ONE

The Camino of Roses

Trish and I were now alone, as Claudia had gone on ahead. We found ourselves walking in a forest and became so engrossed in the beauty around us we missed the turn for the accommodation. It was a stiflingly hot afternoon and we were limping pitifully, having clearly overdone the kilometres. The next accommodation was full, with a stream of people needing help. The angels were summonsed. A van, a promise of a lift to the nearest bed and a lift back in the morning arrived promptly. Trish had heard me talk about St Michael and his vans saving us during other Caminos and she laughed and said, 'Look, Liz. St Michael's van came for us too.'

I had been visualising a bath, and yes we got our wish and spent a wonderful hour bathing our poor feet over the side of the bath. Santiago was nearby. I was feeling excited and yet it was clearly different from the feelings I had in 2010. That trip was so special and had taken so long to finish with so many possible mishaps that could have happened and didn't, which had left me elated with gratitude. This time I was leaving the excitement to Trish as the first time is always special and hard to explain. I felt the Camino of the Roses was telling me to acknowledge the 2010 journey. Every time I quickened my pace my feet complained and I was forced to slow up and smell the roses, keeping my promise to Vinney. He had sent me on this to build on all I had confronted on previous Caminos. He knew I needed to walk it slowly, to fully appreciate the route and the insights from before.

I felt one woman I met was sent to me as an example. Susan was from North America. She was walking to Santiago at a pace of twenty kilometres a day. She was writing about her experiences, taking pictures and chatting to everyone she met. It was certainly a very relaxed way to do the Camino, and I felt someone was telling me something that day. Susan was even sleeping in a tent and cooking her food outdoors. Camping is about surviving earth's elements and feeling safe regardless of the weather, trusting God for everything.

Trish and I met another woman who left her mark on us. Despite being close to Santiago, we were going extremely slow because my feet wouldn't allow me to go any faster. The slow pace didn't disturb us. There is something so special about just sauntering along the road, not sure where one will end up and yet not being concerned. This is probably because she knew it was all part of a plan. The one thing we can be sure of is this Camino and all our Caminos will end. On our last day we will reach our true destination, our summit. And there will be no 'baggage' at this summit. That's why we need to learn how to drop it while we are alive, or we will come back to learn any lessons we missed along the way. Trish wondered how we would know when we had dropped enough baggage. I wasn't entirely sure, but I knew it would involve a feeling of lightness, not a fleeting feeling, one that stays. Within hours of our conversation about baggage, Trish and I encountered another lady, and it was no coincidence.

She looked forty and was over fifty, with the blackest eyes and dark hair and smooth fresh skin and she was from Florida. She told us she was travelling around the world seeing all the places she had ever dreamed of.

'That's amazing. What motivated you to come by yourself?' I asked.

'It was the cancer,' she announced, and I almost got sick at the mention of the word. I try not to think of that ailment that is taking so many people off their life Camino so prematurely. That's what got me thinking of my own experience and the fact that I hid it and put it behind me as if it never happened; it was too scary to bring up. This lady was so open and brave telling us of her diagnosis and the major surgery and then another and a divorce on top of that.

What trauma for one woman and I marvelled at her bravery as she accompanied Trish and me to the restaurant for food. There she told us that after recovering from the surgeries, she made up her mind to sell all her possessions, including her house, her clothes and jewellery. All she had in the world was the small bag on her back. She had read about the Camino and had seen the film *The Way* and decided to find out herself what it was all about.

'You're a vagabond,' I said. 'Just like us.' And we all laughed and began a friendship. She wasn't sure what she would do when she finished her travels, she was leaving that to the universe.

'You are very brave and I have no doubt you will be well looked after by God, and all the angels that surround you. I will keep you in my prayers,' I said.

She thanked me. She was detaching herself from all the 'baggage' that had made her sick, starting afresh in the hope of a full recovery and the beginning of a new Camino. She was also researching her family; she was part Trinidadian and Portuguese with a bit of Scottish heritage thrown in. She wanted to find the gene that was hereditary and made her sick. She was one of the many warriors I met throughout this and other Caminos.

We are all true warriors of light, happy in our adventures. Paulo Coelho describes the warrior of light as being 'never predictable'. Their behaviour is 'quite mad', they sometimes behave like water, flowing around the obstacles they encounter, and in doing so following the light. The warrior of light is always vigilant and is wise enough not to talk about their defeats. They see yesterday's pain as today's strength, which is given by the spark of God within the self. We all speak of the joy in reaching the destinations; very few talk about the struggles in getting there. I silently acknowledged the experience of reliving past times through the forces on the road that could be felt under my feet. Roman soldiers pounding the roads on foot and on horseback; warriors always on a mission embedded in the tapestry of the road.

We were mere kilometres from Santiago and still at a slow pace. I felt St James nearby as he filled my thoughts. He became disheartened on his way to Zaragoza along the Ebro River. He had travelled to Spain and was preaching the gospel with little success. He knelt down and prayed and a great light appeared in front of him; it was the Virgin Mary being carried on a throne surrounded by thousands of angels. She told James that he should persevere, that his efforts would one day be fruitful. She asked that a church be built on the place where she appeared, and St James immediately gathered some of his new followers and began work on a chapel on the designated site. The chapel is the first church ever dedicated to Mary. I admired his perseverance. He has an extremely long legacy and I'm sure there are few that can match his success of spreading the love of God, even after his death.

The Camino of Roses was very special indeed. Walking into the cathedral with Trish in tow, I felt Vinney say, 'It's as you said it was Liz, spectacular.' I had previously explained to him about the cathedral and the exultation you feel when entering it. I sat on the end of a seat watching Trish being hypnotised by the magic of the ambiance and the music. I felt emotional for her, as I was reminded of the first time I entered the cathedral and the great feeling of magic in the air. I was mesmerised then and again now. I felt the deep-seated peace and clarity that radiated into my heart and a roar of gratitude erupted, causing tears to slide onto my clasped hands. It was there and then in that pew after my Camino of Roses that I decided to go to Scotland and erect a new headstone for my parents and the rest of the family interred in the grave that caused me so much trauma as a child. I wanted a place where people could visit and remember them, just as people visit St James and even say a prayer despite, in many cases, not even being religious. I would put a symbol of a white dove on top, representing free spirits: my symbol of freedom to them and peace of mind to the family.

After the Mass and the majestic singing we were floating on air, and I was wondering where we could stay. My sore feet were acting up as I limped out of the cathedral and into the square. Trish and I stood in the square looking about in amazement at all the pilgrims arriving by bike, on foot and even by horse and cart. Some were limping, being led by others, like wounded soldiers. Most of the pilgrims stood in awe at the scale of the building, profound emotion showing on their faces. Some dropped to their knees in gratitude for a safe journey. I felt tears well up and heard my father say, 'Well done. You made it, sore feet and all.' My senses were at a whole new high.

A nice young man with a smile that reached his eyes asked if we wanted to go inside the seminary, a beautiful building previously used for priests to live and study right beside the cathedral.

'Would you like to stay here?' he asked as he took my arm and led us inside. There were two adjacent rooms available for two nights with dinner and breakfast for a very reasonable fee. This building is normally full and booked only on the internet. St James and Vinney certainly had the Camino of the Roses planned to the very last step. It was there that I rested my sore feet and almost immediately they began to heal. Throughout this journey, I wondered why I had such sore feet, and the answer I believe comes from Archangel Metatron. This is the angel that helps us to be grounded by bringing us back to our roots by balancing our chakras, in particular our root chakra, which helps us focus and frees us of any emotions that are holding us back.

The Camino of the Roses was coming to an end. Trish and I decided to take the bus to Finisterre, to the end of the earth. In the old days people went to burn their clothes and start afresh, to free themselves of 'baggage'. As soon as I put my feet into the sea, they began to heal and the swelling reduced, so much so I was able to walk to the airport from Santiago to catch the plane home, all the 'baggage' left in the foundations on the road. That serenity gave me a sense of wanting to dance with life and share the experience with the whole world. But first we were to have a few of our own celebrations in Finisterre.

We are sitting in a fine fish restaurant, reading the menu, and Trish was complaining that the wine the previous night had kept her awake. Minutes later, when the waitress came to take our order, she asked Trish if she wanted water or wine.

'I'll have the wine, please,' she replied, and we both dissolved with laughter.

We were the only ones in the restaurant, looking out onto the sea, into the complete darkness with only the stars for light. Suddenly I overheard the manager tell the waitress to smile at her customers, which I thought was very odd. I looked closely at her then and saw a hollowness in her eyes; she seemed miles away. When I smiled at her, she tried hard to smile back, but tears filled her eyes. She produced a picture of her dad in a hospital bed, linked up to tubes, and she said he had died the previous month. She also said she had lost her unborn baby in the same month. That picture reminded me of my father when he was ill and it stirred up old memories that unsettled me. My heart went out to her. It is those left behind who carry the trauma of death and sometimes the baggage that comes with it. We think of unspoken words or anger we may have had towards that person who died, or maybe we are crippled by the loneliness and heartbreak that death brings. The angels, saints and family rejoice on their return. One of my dreams on another Camino was of all my family sitting in a circle and they seemed to be waiting and rejoicing. I had woken with a start and wondered what it was about. It wasn't long after that night that my brother passed away in his sleep and my aunt Rosie the following month and a few more people after that. It never stopped till November when Vinney joined them. That was 2014 and I'm grateful that I haven't had a year like that since. Frankly, I don't think I would have been able for the strain. I believe God will only give us what we are able for at one sitting.

Suddenly, I remembered the beautiful twelfth-century church Trish and I had entered along the Camino. The windows told the story of St Francis and his journey with God. Trish had also been moved, realising that St Francis was accompanying us. The smell of the wood and dust was hypnotic and when I closed my eyes I was transported right back into the century it had been built. An old man approached us while we sat there. He had soft blue eyes and wispy grey hair. He handed me a little prayer with a picture of Our Lady on it. He was sweet and hugged me tight. I wasn't sure why he had given it to me as it was in Spanish, but looking at this young waitress in front of me, I knew it was for her. I took the prayer out of my pouch and handed it to her.

She looked at it, kissed it, and said, 'For me?'

'Yes,' I replied, 'for you'.

She hugged me and held it to her heart while wiping her tears. 'Thank you. I will keep it always,' she said, staring at the picture as if I had given her a thousand pounds. It never fails to amaze me that such a small gesture can give so much pleasure and security to people in need of guidance. It almost instantly releases stress and lightens someone's burden.

My grandmother sent me a similar picture of the Madonna and child in 1974. I arrived in Dublin at the age of eighteen, newly married with a sense of wonder, and loneliness for the family. I was in a strange country, and I may as well have been on the moon such was the strangeness of the city. Granny wrote, 'Keep this always. I had it for years. I hope it will help you always. All my love, Granny.'

She knew I would need Our Lady in my life just as much as she did, and I have always prayed to her and believed she walks with me. It is a gift and a privilege to know we are not alone, even in the darkest days, or on the highest mountain or the loneliest nights. To know there is a source greater than us and someday we will be part of that source, is sustaining. That picture of Our Lady gave the waitress solace.

As I write this I have a better understanding of this would, and all its ups and downs, that keep us on our toes, and try us in the most difficult of ways. Without prayer, I would not be walking in peace on this Camino, of that I'm sure. I'm so grateful for all the help I get from my angels and guides that walk with me. And I wasn't done with the Camino just yet either. I knew deep in my soul there was another itch to scratch. Fully relaxed, back in Dublin after the Camino of Roses, Mary and I decided to do another one, this time on foot. We were heading for the Camino of Portugal.

CHAPTER TWENTY-TWO

The Portuguese Camino –

July 2017

*'A human being, who trusts in God's strength, has an endless love for his
fellow beings'*

I packed and unpacked at least five times, thinking of the journey
ahead and pondering on the freedom to walk the way, once again, as
the poor donkey, only this time there would be very little to carry.
We would take the bare essentials and trust in all the earth angels that
we would meet en route. Co-existence with all people past and present
and the uncertainty of each day and what it would bring – that thought
gave me great joy and a sense of excitement. One thing I was sure of
was that St Michael, St Francis, St Teresa and Padre Pio and any other
saint that came to mind would not rest till we were safely back on the
plane for home.

The Portuguese Camino is known as the spiritual route, the route of
St James where they brought his body across by boat from Jerusalem
to bury it. We decided to start in Porto and just walk, not looking for
anything in particular or to reach Santiago or kill ourselves en route. We
did not need another indulgence, just some exercise, fresh air and time to
spend together. But I had a feeling this would turn out to be an adventure
with spiritual guidance. The Portuguese Camino is the second most

popular Camino in terms of numbers of pilgrims heading to Santiago. This way starts in the colourful UNESCO-listed city of Porto and it's a fascinating route, moving past seaside towns and villages in northern Portugal. We knew that St James's feast day, 25 July, was a week away and I wondered if I'd get my wish to be in Santiago for that day. I also knew, of course, that we shouldn't rush and invite struggle and pain.

We began at a tiny little church on the coast that had a large stone with St Francis written on it. That place was once a Franciscan church. I marvelled at how quickly St Francis made himself known to us once again. The beautiful foamy waves tapped at the rocks and the sun pelted down, causing sweat to pile up on my forehead. I knew then this could be our enemy, and we would have to be careful to shelter when it was at its hottest. With this in mind we started out on our walk. There is a boardwalk winding around the coast making it easier on the feet. After six hours of strolling and laughing and deciding what next, as we both wanted to get to Santiago, we landed at a monastery of St Clare, the first Franciscan nun to follow in St Francis' footsteps. This was a beautiful building built in the twelfth century. We circled it and stared at the statues and thanked St Clare and all the angels for a safe journey.

That night I settled into one of eight bunk beds in a small room. I lay in the dark and contemplated the day, dozing off into a dream where I was laughing and sitting on a seat with my father. It's unreal how one can be transported into another time or place. I felt he was happy and at peace; there was a beautiful feeling coming from him and I felt it was love. I awoke in the knowledge that he had depleted his 'baggage' and had forgiven himself for his poor choices in this life. The fact that I had cleared out my baggage of all the times I hated him as a child, when he and the world were both strange and scary, left him with a free spirit. I felt all the unwanted 'baggage' was left on the Camino of Roses when my feet were sore and the issues in my tissues went back into the earth, mixing among the roots of the trees and the foundations of the earth. Now he could grow in the spirit world, moving up in line, reaching perfection, leaving him ready to come back onto the planet to do good deeds for the people and the earth. His serenity in heaven gave me serenity on earth and I wept with joy, for the indulgence I said in his name had helped free his soul.

My message to people from this experience is to dig deep. We can heal ourselves and drop the 'baggage' we carry close to our hearts by lifting the flag that holds back the joy. There are happy moments and they will rise up from among the debris, given half a chance. It's fear that holds them back, fear someone might notice we are upset and think we are actually normal. There is not one person on this planet that has not carried 'baggage' of some sort in their lifetime. Let it go, do it, bit by bit, when you are ready, like clearing out a loved one's closet and wanting to hold onto everything because they owned them and feeling guilty if you let them go.

Feeling the freedom of spirit gives us power we can use to help and love.

The next part of the spiritual journey was similar to the unexpected one that took us through the forest in France where my chain snapped with a warning from St Michael that virtually saved my life. This memory gave me such gratitude, knowing he had the trip planned and there would be nothing to worry about. Walking through the vibrant forest opened all the senses and left a peaceful melody within my heart. The butterflies were in abundance and seemed to mock us as if to say, 'Look at you, on the road again, giving us such joy knowing you are happy and trusting us for guidance.'

A stream ran alongside us. The water lapping on the banks of the forest made us feel at home. There was a smell of roses that reminded me of my friend Vinney and the Camino of Roses; he was right there with us again. I took my shoes off and dipped my feet into the running water, which reminded me of when I was a child. I loved to sit and watch the water running from a stream in my grandmother's backyard. There was an abundance of wildlife flying about there too and I noticed the butterflies were dancing over the water, spit-firing in front of us. The pace was slow, giving us time to reflect and be in the moment and full of gratitude. I was full sure we would not have one bit of bother even if we lost the map.

We had developed so much faith it was reassuring. There was a time I would have been wary of who came along and afraid to sleep, like my friend Trish was in Pietrelcina in northern Italy when we went to see Padre Pio's place of birth. Strange things happened on that path. We accidently strayed off the rosary road. It was like the place was haunted and full of noises that actually latched onto my phone and sounded like a monster when played back, which freaked us out no end. So much so Trish had all the pictures of Padre Pio around her in the bed and she prayed all night and never slept a wink. The Camino spiritual route was unlike the rest of the routes because of all the mishaps and storms that happened on them. Regardless of how bad the incident was, we were safe every time. In fact, we always landed in a little piece of heaven with kind people in the form of earth angels to take care of us.

The next part of our route finished in a monastery at the end of the river. A restful night awaited us, including delicious food. There was so much, it took us two hours to eat and drink. After looking around the beautiful Franciscan monastery, we received a lovely Mass, beautifully delivered by a little monk. He could have been St Francis himself, such was his humbleness as he said the prayers among the ancient artefacts representing St Francis. That night in my bed in the little cell that had housed monks for centuries, I prayed that more people would walk the Camino and receive the daily grace awaiting them.

St James's remains were brought across the Arousa estuary and up the Ulla River until reaching Iria Flavia (now the village of Padrón) from Jerusalem. A boat now takes pilgrims along this water route following his journey. That's where we wanted to go and the anniversary was playing havoc within our minds. We both knew what the other was thinking and we just knew we would get there. We continued on the path surrounded by the water. It was to take the whole day and most of the night and we promised we would not rush. I said a prayer to St Michael and my father to help us if we needed assistance on route, for I wasn't going all night and accommodation on that Camino is scarce and far between.

Having walked in peace and serenity by the river, listening to the wildlife with no other people about, our feet talking to us and a rumble like a volcano heard coming from our tummies that frightened the birds, we knew it was time to stop. But where? There was no one about and no heavy traffic on the very narrow road, with the tiniest little roundabout I had ever seen on the Camino. We stood in silence wondering what next, when out of nowhere a young girl with radiant black eyes and dark wavy hair reading a book appeared in front of us. She looked up, smiled and asked where we were going. She was from Mexico and we tried to explain where we wanted to get to.

'Show her the map, Mary,' I said, thinking it was the first time I had requested the map on all the journeys to date. 'We want to get to Villanova,' I said.

She said she lived close by and offered to bring us to the albergue in her car. Once again, St Michael was at work. I sat their dog on my lap and we chatted about our journey and found out her husband was Portuguese and she Mexican. I got that weird feeling of familiarity again, like I had met them before. I was once told by a person who reads auras that I had a spirit guide from a Mayan village in Mexico. She said he was a soulmate that has been with me all my life. She told me I should ask him for help when I was in need.

A very nice accommodation awaited us. The albergue was in a large school hall. The bottom half was full of teenagers playing basketball, while the upper half was decorated as an albergue with room for more than twenty people, with everything we needed for washing, cooking and a rest room with a volunteer manager who loved what he did. He had a glow about him that showed spiritual awareness. He sat us down and showed us a video on the route of St James, the journey on the boat that replicated the one used to mimic the route used to bring St James's body across by his pilgrims. He also had the information and tickets for the boat to Padrón. We were following in his footsteps and would end up passing the village called Pilar. A church was built on the very spot where Our Lady appeared to St James in Pilar. Mary appeared to him in his darkest confusing days. There was a great sense of excitement going on among the pilgrims and I had a magical sense that more excitable and perhaps unexplainable incidents would happen to us en route.

I had a strong sense there was something in the pipeline and it would be revealed in time! We were after all just as much an apostle to St James as he was to Jesus. St James, along with other apostles, fell asleep when Jesus asked them to stay awake. We are all asleep at times, living in the past afraid to move on, living in fear or even guilt that haunts our consciousness, and sadly we are not even aware of them. Earth angels on the Camino have shown me that we are all capable of good deeds and our job on this Camino is also to help people by showing them love and understanding when we get an opportunity.

We found ourselves in a boat among a large group of pilgrims in Villanova on 24 July. Excitement and banter rose among us as we watched the sun come up over the horizon, replacing the moon that had kept watch all night. A gentle wind blew around us causing us to huddle together. I thanked God I hadn't had breakfast, as my stomach was churning from the waves. Once off the boat, we marched purposefully to the church in Pilar. We stood looking, disappointment written on Mary's face and I felt it in my bones – all this way and it was closed.

After a full day of walking and us roughly ten kilometres from Santiago de Compostela, we needed to find accommodation. I had dreamt of a large wild-looking garden and I felt we would end up there at the end of the day. We decided it being the day before the anniversary of St James and it being late on in the day, it would be unwise to try for accommodation in the city. A long stretch of what looked like a wild garden surrounded by trees lay before us; it was a replica of my dream. There was a recommended five-star restaurant and an accommodation attached and we headed inside. A nice young man brought us up to the one free room.

'Well, you got your garden, Liz,' said Mary.

Unpacked and showered, we both felt tired and we lay in the darkened room. I thought I would watch Mary fall asleep and I would contemplate the day. But I was more than surprised when almost immediately I went into a deep sleep, where I was transported back into a long, wild garden. The most magnificent of visitations I have had to date happened to me. I was accompanied by Our Lady; the feeling was so beautiful and it felt so right. We walked together side by side and she pointed to a church. I awoke a little startled and could remember every little detail.

Mary woke up and she said, 'I thought you were out. I heard you go and I thought you went into the garden because you wanted to see it.'

'I did go, Mary, and it was beautiful. I can hardly believe what happened. There is a church in that garden. I was transported there in a vision and what an experience I had. I walked beside Our Lady. She was beautiful and radiated pure love and I knew it came from her heart. God I'm so lucky on the Camino and so blessed in life itself.'

We both walked into the garden. There were local people cutting down trees and some fixing cars. We headed down the back and came across a beautiful old early-twelfth-century church. As it happened, there was a lady inside cleaning and arranging candles at the altar. She said it rarely opened, only on feast days and Christmas holidays. We sat and looked at two very old wooden statues standing alongside each other: St James and Our Lady. We got our wish to see them together. The cleaner handed us pictures of St James and we slipped them into our bags. I was elated. I knew that journey would complete the journey that Margaret Solis said I would do. It also gave me solace knowing Our

Lady, whom I loved dearly ever since I first heard about her when I was seven years old, was still with me. I wasn't imagining things all the times I heard her and felt her standing by me both on the Camino and before I ever knew about the Camino.

The decision was made to forget the fireworks and the night-time celebrations for St James's feast day. It was late into the night, and we had no way of travelling into the city, one disadvantage of not having the bike at hand. With a slight bit of sadness we ate our locally grown vegetables and hot and spicy fish and prawns. We washed it down with a glass of wine to toast the saint. A couple from London were eating their food and heard us talk about the journey. John and Janet were travelling around Spain and read about Santiago and decided to see for themselves what the excitement was about. They asked us to join them and said they were driving into the city for the fireworks. We were overjoyed.

While chatting to John, en route to the city, he told me that Janet had had breast cancer surgery on 13 July 2008. I felt startled at this information at first and unsure how to respond. My mind was racing and I said, 'That's ironic, so did I, and it was Friday the thirteenth, unlucky for some, but for us it was more than luck.'

'What made you tell me that news?' I asked him.

'I don't know,' he replied. 'It just came out and it's strange. I don't normally talk about that time or the fact that I have just come through treatment myself,' he went on to say. 'We have to look on the positive side, don't you think?' he said, looking at his arms where the skin had changed colour and become patchy, the results of the treatment.

'It's a strange place is the Camino, lots of things happen we can't understand,' I said. I told him how I believed all the angels and spirits that surround us are right here on the Camino, walking in our footsteps, waiting to help us should we get lost. That's my conclusion of the Camino. I could feel my father close by us. It was the smell of smoke; he never fails to get my attention with it. I have been smelling them for years and I wish he would stop, they make me sick.

'Can you smell the smoke here?' I asked John, who looked at me as if my brain was sizzled. 'I believe my father is also celebrating St James's feast day. After all, they have both been making their presence known every day we have been on the Camino. Just as Margaret Solis predicted they would,' I said to him. 'And I'll tell you about her after the fireworks are over.'

We both laughed and set about enjoying the night sky light up with hundreds of fireworks surrounded by thousands of pilgrims from all over the world, singing and dancing. There they were, celebrating a man they never knew much about, except he was real and had feelings and fears just like them. St James had cried with confusion and prayed for strength and direction until Our Lady appeared to reassure him. His job was to bring pilgrims together to find their purpose in life in Santiago. I wonder what our journey is all about? Are we meant to share our stories about Santiago and the Camino experiences? That's what I have been wondering for a long time now.

'What do you think, John?' I asked.

'You sure have a lot to share and I feel it would help others on their Camino,' he replied, 'and I for one would be most interested to read them.'

The last leg into Santiago was slow and meticulous. We walked in silence, each of us in our own thoughts. The bag felt light indeed and my feet felt like brand new. My heart was free and singing with joy as we stepped into the cathedral in time for the special Mass at midday on the 25 July. We had done it! We had got our long-awaited wish to celebrate the feast day in the cathedral of Santiago. There was a mad dash for seats and I thought we would have to stand, when Mary squeezed in beside a crowd and I sat between a middle-aged man and some young people a row behind her. Sitting back to watch the incense swing back and forward, the scent made me dizzy with satisfaction. I smiled to myself and sat back to enjoy the sermon. At first I thought he was just sniffling, that he had a cold, until I looked at the middle-aged gentleman beside me and saw a tear leave his eye and a deep heartfelt sigh leave his body. He was looking intently at the altar, trying to hide his distress by swallowing his sobs, almost choking himself in the process.

I asked Jesus for guidance on what to do. I looked at him and smiled, and he looked back with vacant eyes and tears running down his face. He began to sob, great big sobs racking his body. I reached over and took his hand and squeezed it tight. 'It's okay,' I said reassuringly. 'It's okay.' He sobbed again. Tears gathered in my eyes and I joined him and we both sobbed and he squeezed my hand and I felt a sense of love for this strange little man. He seemed to be lonely and lost. I reached inside my pouch and took out the picture of the apostle Santiago I had acquired in the old church in the garden. I placed it in his hand. He looked at it and placed it on his chest and said, 'Apostle, apostle, apostle.' He kissed it and held it close to his chest, looked at me and reached out to give it back. I shook my head and told him it was for him. He shook his head in disbelief – it was as if no one had ever given him a gift before. I got up to go to the altar and he stood waiting for me to return. He stood aside to let me past and squeezed my hand. Tears ran freely down his cheeks, causing me to almost choke with emotion. The time came to wish each other 'Peace be with you' and we looked at each other. He reached out and hugged me tight, kissing my cheeks. Mary looked around to shake hands and she told me later that all she could see was this middle-aged man hugging and kissing me. When the sermon was over he kept thanking me and hugging me. All I could see in his eyes was my father; it was such a strange experience. He was communicating to me through the nice man. That feeling is hard to describe; it was one of peace and tranquillity that went deep into my soul as I waved him goodbye. That was the last time I smelled smoke and felt my father around me. I felt he was saying 'Thanks, for setting my soul free and understanding what I was trying to say to you.'

As we walked to the accommodation, I looked at the abundance of roses growing out of the bushes surrounding the trees. It reminded me of the Camino of Roses and my friend Vinney.

I know they are still watching me from behind the mirror, free spirits.

Life's a journey and not a destination and we are all on a Camino – that's the main lesson I learned while travelling around the Camino. There is no point in carrying 'baggage' from one generation to another. Drop the 'baggage' while we are here. It is no good to us, not one bit of it. It will only make us sick. Another important thing I realised was that, no matter how much we worry or how far we travel, we are never alone. When we are anxious or afraid, all we have to do is ask for an angel and it will be granted. On all the roads and mountains I travelled any one of them could have been the last, and I am entirely grateful to be able to write this down in the hope that someone will take the courage and set out on a Camino with a few necessary pieces of 'baggage' and a free spirit. One sets out as a tourist and ends up as a pilgrim on the Camino.

CHAPTER TWENTY-THREE

The Heart Is a Temple of Love

'The heart is a temple of love.'

— VINCENT CROWLEY

I have always been haunted by dreams and the Camino has helped me understand them as being 'messages from spirit'. One message I received in November 2014, the night before my dear friend Vincent's burial, was this. He came to me smiling and he held my hand out and put two halves of a ring on my finger on my right hand. The ring was silver with rugged edges that came together to fit perfectly, like two halves of a heart making one. As he put them there he said the words, 'The heart is a temple of love.' I awoke with tears running down my face and repeated his words, 'The heart is a temple of love.' That was his message to me and I feel I am meant to share it as he was a powerful man who loved God. He had a gentle heart that was easily broken. I am so glad he enticed me to smell the roses and continue the journey we had planned, which was to walk the Camino and to take our time to smell the roses.

The heart holds love and can be easily broken from pain and suffering, leaving us traumatised. Fear can set in, telling us to 'close the heart and protect it from pain'. If we close the heart to pain, we close it to love, and we will live on shielding ourselves and missing out on all the love that may come our way. I believe my father closed his heart and was innately afraid to open it; he was afraid of the pain he carried until the day he died. What he failed to see is that love comes in many forms. It can be as simple as a smile or a nod from a stranger when you are feeling low, the comfort of a handshake when the mind is muddled and confused following some tribulations. With a closed heart, your eyes cannot see the sun after the storm because clouds hang like curtains veiling hope, love and beauty. God's love shines in every storm and in every rainbow and we should relish them all.

I believe the heart can sometimes be broken beyond repair. In the case of soulmates, one part of the soul can pine for the other until eventually the pain becomes so great they let go, releasing all to God, begging him for reconciliation; and he being a noble father relents, and they too join their beloved. Death can be tragic for all the people left behind, and yet the gates of heaven are open causing a roar of joy and a chorus of singing from all the saints and the angels and the family and soulmates, waiting to greet them. We, the people left behind, have to get strength in knowing there is one more guide to help us live with the loneliness death brings.

I believe Vinney died of a broken heart shortly after his beloved wife passed away. I believe they were soulmates who are now at the summit, with God and the angels. I also believe that one person can wait for another to bring them home after they die.

When a very dear friend of mine named Ann died, it was a big shock for me, as we were kindred spirits. She had two daughters, and after she died I wondered how one of them would cope without her; the other I felt would manage. I'm not sure why, but it was a feeling I had as they had a very tight bond. In 2006 Ann came to me in my sleep in the Himalayas and she was joyful and told me she was waiting. I thought she was waiting for me until a few months later her daughter was killed on a bike while out training. Then I understood what she was saying, and a few weeks after her departure she came again and told me she was going home and her daughter was rowing her boat. That message was confirmed by a spiritual teacher named Maharaja. I listened to him talk about this life and the fact that we are all on a boat and what we do while on the boat is important. Sometimes that boat will be smooth and sometimes it will rock, and we need to be able for all weathers to survive this Camino. Someday someone will come to sail us home and we will be part of the ocean. That message helped me understand why some people die close to others, especially people they were very close to in this life even if they were very young.

Soulmates come in many forms and can be spouses, children or friends. From my journey on the Camino I learned that people we meet, are close to or are having difficulty with are all part of past lives and perhaps we have journeys that are not complete and we need to learn more of what the true meaning of life is. We must also know where we came from, the generations that came before. One of my regrets in life is that I could not keep my promise to my aunt to bring her back to Ireland to be reunited with her family. But I now realise that some things are not meant to be. It was her time, just as it was for my mother when her untimely death came about, that was her time, and they both had a purpose in this lifetime, just as we have. It was the way their deaths were preserved and the unveiling of the secret that had haunted us, that caused the deep-seated confusion and hurt to us children, especially with my mother. We knew nothing of her, not even her birthday, and every photograph I had seen was black and white. I didn't even know the colour of her eyes. The only things we had belonging to her were a marriage certificate and a death certificate, and neither had her birthdate on it. I decided to find out for myself and set off on a trail around the churches and searched the books until I found out. Some people will say 'let sleeping dogs lie' as in leave well alone and don't shake up the past. But if the dog is sleeping and not dead, it is impossible to let it lie, for it will at some point raise its head.

The Camino was unravelling so much in my body and mind was is hard to believe there was so much stored. If this 'baggage' is not identified and acknowledged it will sit quietly like the sleeping dog or worse a sleeping volcano. Volcanos can with time erupt and surprise us with the amount of debris that spills out. I'm glad I was on the Camino when this happened, for I have had time to acknowledge and realise the main storage point. The heart is the main storage point of pain. It is also the storage point of love; having love in any form overrides the pain and the heart will heal and allow more love to enter, should we allow it. That task gave both myself and my siblings peace of mind and unravelled part of a mystery.

Every time my aunt Lilly sang 'Galway Bay' a great sadness came over her. I recognised this as I grew older and I made a promise to one day go and see what made her so sad. I kept my promise, and it is one of the most magnificent sights I have seen to date. It was a glorious sunset, a ball of fire leaving the sky majestically slipping into the ocean in Galway Bay. There were flames of bright orange and vibrant red that would blind you with their beauty. I cried watching that beautiful sight in her honour, and I knew she wanted me to find her family.

My husband, sister and I set off in the car to a village called Belturbet in Co. Cavan. While watching a very old nun leave a convent, I remembered my aunt telling me she had worked for nuns when she was young. I asked my sister to go over and ask the nun if she had known our aunt and where her family lived. She did. It took me fifteen years to go and answer that persistent voice, but when I did, it was like a weight had been lifted from my soul and I knew my aunt was finally happy. Her family hadn't known what had happened to her and to us children after my mother died. I found and developed a wonderful relationship with two of her sisters and I was privileged to hold one of their hands at the great age of eighty-nine when she took her last breath. Her name was Rosie. I felt God was rewarding me for finding her and making up for not being able to acknowledge my mother in death. I got the chance to whisper the rosary into her ear. I've no doubt there was a gang waiting for her with open arms at the summit.

I believe I'm blessed in having had people in my life that looked out for me when I was a child, showing love in a silent hug that touched my heart, never seeking reward – that to me is unconditional love, and my aunt was full of it. I was deprived of my mother, but having her sister was a privilege and a blessing.

My life has been a gift. It has been full of hurdles in the form of mountains, all of which challenged and rewarded me. The higher they were the more challenging they became and the more determined I was to cross them. These challenges can only be done with the help of God and the angels, and, of course, true guts, discipline and determination. Everybody can achieve 'great things' if they really want to, but they must first stop blaming their lives on their upbringing and their parents or lack of parenting – 'baggage' must be discarded.

Karma is what we carry from one generation to another and I believe in order to break karma we need to forgive from the heart and free the soul that wants to come back onto the planet and complete a journey with a fresh start. The soul that is fresh and holds no 'baggage' will be a mighty soul doing great deeds for the people and the planet. That's my thought and I hope if we can open our heart to peace and forgiveness that, when our time comes to leave this wonderful planet, we can meet St Peter with open arms and be sent straight to the summit, running to meet all those who wait to greet us.

Some people get lost on their Camino, while others, like my father, get stuck at a crossroads. His inability to free his heart and lift his flag and see all the beauty and love he still had, left us stuck too. But as he accompanied me along my Camino, regardless of my initial denial of him, he persisted because I needed to hear a message: you need to be free of baggage in order to run to the light.

When I started to write this I had this deep feeling of anguish, as I felt people may read it and they would judge both me for hating my father and him for his mistakes. I'm not saying it is easy and automatic to just let go. It's not. First you need to find the 'baggage' and then dig deep and pull everything and let it go. St Michael can help here as he has the power to cut the cords that attach us to the past. All we need to do is meditate and visualise him around us with his bright sword, moving slowly cutting the cords one by one and releasing us of trauma we don't need. When we do this we will get messages in our dreams and in our waking days that will help us move on. We need to look for the guidance and the symbols and move forward fearlessly. Don't be afraid of what lies at the top of the mountain, nor how steep the descent might be.

The joy is in the reward and the sense of freedom and lightness that frees the heart, leaving it open and ready for love. Open your heart; hear your heartbeat. It can roar like a lion in the silence, reminding us to be gentle with ourselves. The heart is a temple of love, for yourself, for others and for those who have passed on. The secret is cherishing your heartbeat and living each day as the gift it is. I am grateful for all the love and guidance I have received from my family, friends, the angels and saints – all who have accompanied me on my Camino.

Life is a journey and not a destination.
Every breath is sacred and should be
Relished like a precious gem, for
Death comes like a storm in the night.

— ELIZABETH MCKENNA